Economics in Action

14 Greatest Hits for Teaching High School Economics

Editors

Jane S. Lopus

Amy M. Willis

Created through a partnership between the
National Council on Economic Education and **Junior Achievement Japan**

NCEE

National Council on Economic Education

Junior -Japan-
Achievement®

Generous funding for this publication was provided by
the **Citigroup Foundation**

Editors:

Jane S. Lopus
Professor of Economics
Director, Center for Economic Education
California State University, Hayward

Amy M. Willis
Economics Teacher
Desert Mountain High School, Scottsdale, Arizona
Program Director
Arizona Council on Economic Education

Project Editor: Melinda Patterson Grenier

Design: Karl Hartig

Illustration: Roger Roth

ISBN   1-56183-086-0   5 4 3 2

Contents

Foreword

The National Council on Economic Education (NCEE) is delighted to partner with Junior Achievement Japan to publish *Economics in Action*. We also are grateful to the Citigroup Foundation for making this publication possible in both Japanese and English.

For over 53 years NCEE has been publishing instructional materials that actively engage students in lessons that demonstrate important economic concepts and the economic reasoning process. These lessons provide students with an introduction to the core ideas in the Voluntary National Content Standards in Economics developed under the leadership of NCEE. The standards are designed to help students make more informed economic choices as consumers, employees, and citizens. Most importantly, these lessons utilize active-learning techniques. The students take part in simulations, group decision making, problem solving, classroom demonstrations, role-plays, and group presentations. The students learn by doing.

Economics in Action represents the best of NCEE's activity-based economics lessons. The 14 lessons in this collection are all-time favorites of lessons previously published by NCEE. Versions of these lessons have been used throughout the United States and in many other parts of the world. We are grateful to the authors who created these lessons over the years.

In *Economics in Action*, Jane Lopus, Director of the California State University-Hayward Center for Economic Education, and Amy Willis, Program Director of the Arizona Council on Economic Education, have built on this past work and have taken these lessons to an even higher level. Teachers will find the lessons a pleasure to use, and students will be actively engaging their minds in economic thinking while enjoying the ride. We hope these lessons are just the beginning of their journey to economic literacy.

Robert F. Duvall, Ph.D.
President and Chief Executive Officer
National Council on Economic Education

Foreword

As we stand on the brink of a global economic system, it is essential for all of us to understand how our society is structured and how the economy works. Young people particularly need a firm base to help them plan their lives if they are to become fully-fledged members of society after leaving school. Economics, however, has long been considered one of the more difficult academic subjects by middle and high school teachers, and this has led to a noticeable lack of enthusiasm about teaching economics. This is one of the major reasons why economic literacy is not well developed in our society.

I believe the best way to improve this situation is to allow teachers to develop confidence or interest in teaching economics by providing them with practical teaching tools, such as a teacher's manual containing various hands-on lessons on economic issues. Junior Achievement Japan and the National Council on Economic Education agreed to cooperate in a partnership to combine both organizations' knowledge and expertise for this purpose. The results of the first joint project of these two organizations is this teacher's manual, *Economics in Action*.

This manual will allow teachers, who may not have sound knowledge of economics, to feel relatively comfortable and enthusiastic about teaching economics in the classroom. I strongly believe that only by combining the knowledge of both of these two leading organizations can we create the best quality programs and materials that will allow young people to acquire practical economic knowledge and skills.

This teacher's manual, *Economics in Action*, is in Japanese and English for teachers of both languages, but I sincerely hope it will be translated into other languages and contribute to developing mutual understanding among nations around the world.

Takeo Shiina
Chairman of the Board of Directors
for Junior Achievement Japan
Senior Advisor of IBM Japan, Ltd.

Acknowledgments

Most of the lessons in this collection have been compiled, and in some cases adapted, from earlier publications by the National Council on Economic Education, New York, N.Y. The NCEE lessons originally or previously appeared in the following books:

Advanced Placement Economics, 1996
Capstone: The Nation's High School Economics Course, 1989
Civics and Government: Focus on Economics, 1996
Economics and the Environment, 1996
Economics and the Environment: EcoDetectives, 1997
Focus: High School Economics, First Edition, 1996
Focus: High School Economics, Second Edition, 2001
From Plan to Market, 1997
Geography: Focus on Economics, 1996
The Great Economic Mysteries Book, 9-12, 2000
Master Curriculum Guide in Economics: Teaching Strategies 5-6, 1994

These publications are available from the National Council on Economic Education. For information on these and other NCEE publications, call toll-free 800-338-1192 to obtain a catalog or view the online catalog at www.ncee.net.

Parts of Lesson 6 and Lesson 13 originally appeared in publications that are no longer in print.

Introduction: **Activity-Based Economics**

Welcome to *Economics in Action*, a compilation of 14 popular lessons that use a variety of activities to teach economics.

Teaching high school economics can be challenging for many reasons. Some teachers are not well prepared in the subject matter and find that developing high-quality lessons is not easy. Also, because the economics course is frequently offered to second-semester seniors, merely keeping students involved and interested can be difficult. And too often students think economics is a dismal science: a dry subject full of complicated graphs and boring examples.

However, economics can be the most relevant and stimulating class students take in high school. One way to make this happen is to actively involve students in lessons that demonstrate important economic concepts and economic reasoning.

The 14 lessons in this collection are all-time favorites from earlier publications by the National Council on Economic Education. The lessons are not intended to stand alone as the course materials; they are recommended as supplements to a good high school economics textbook, as well as to lectures that emphasize content. Activity-based economics is only one tool in the economics teacher's tool kit of instructional methodologies. These lessons can also be used in other high school social-studies classes such as government and history.

The philosophy behind the methodology of *Economics in Action* may be found in this Chinese proverb: "I hear and I forget. I see and I remember. I do and I understand." When students approach the study of economics by doing something that challenges them to use economic reasoning to examine economic behavior, they are more likely to truly understand the concept being taught and why it is important for them. Rote memorization may

provide the appearance of cognition, but actions verify this understanding. As one Japanese student commented after completing Lesson 1 ("Why People Trade"): "Before this lesson, I did not understand well what the teacher taught us about why we trade. However, after this lesson, the answer just fell into my heart."

The most obvious aspect of activity-based economics is that the students are actively engaged in the lessons: They take part in different types of simulations, group decision making, problem solving, classroom demonstrations, role-plays and group presentations. The students are doing, not just hearing and seeing.

Equally important, however, is that the students' minds are actively engaged. Economics is more than a bundle of concepts. Economics is a unique way of thinking that offers insights into the seemingly chaotic behavior that results from different values, resources and cultures. It is a new lens through which students can view the world. According to John Maynard Keynes, "The Theory of Economics does not furnish a body of settled conclusions immediately applicable to policy. It is a method rather than a doctrine, an apparatus of the mind, a technique of thinking that helps its possessor to draw correct conclusions." (Quoted in Paul Heyne, *The Economic Way of Thinking*, 7th ed., New York: Macmillan Publishing Co., 1994, p. 4). Activity-based economics helps teachers use an active-learning methodology and the economic way of thinking to teach important economic concepts and content.

Active-Learning Methodology

The rationale for using active learning is firmly based in pedagogical theory and research. Active, participatory lessons are effective in helping students remember and apply abstract concepts. Different levels of students – from underachievers through honors students – can take part, succeed and benefit from the activities. Group interaction and cooperative-learning methods, which encourage social growth as well as cognition, are emphasized. In addition to the pedagogical rationale for using active learning, students enjoy learning economics this way and become more interested in the subject matter. So do their teachers.

All 14 lessons in *Economics in Action* contain one or more activities requiring students to do more than just passively absorb facts and information. In fact, the activity-based approach challenges students to take responsibility for their own learning. For example, Lesson 4 engages students in observing how property rights affect behavior and then helps them develop conclusions about environmental problems. Lesson 7 allows students to participate as buyers and sellers in a market and experience the laws of supply and demand in action instead of looking only at supply-and-demand graphs and tables. Lesson 11 lets students take part in short auctions that reveal the relationship between inflation and the money supply rather than listening to the teacher talk about this relationship. In Lesson 12, students write a play to show the intent of fiscal policy; and in Lesson 13, they role-play a lazy brother and energetic sister to learn about comparative advantage.

The Economic Way of Thinking
Social sciences seek to explain and analyze human behavior, and economics is no exception. The study of economics revolves around a way of thinking, a way of making choices and evaluating decisions. All 14 lessons in this volume contain an introductory section on economic reasoning and how it relates to the concepts and activities in the lesson. All lessons focus either directly or indirectly on the economic way of thinking.

Active learning is an ideal way to teach the economic way of thinking. When students participate in activities requiring them to make choices and decisions, they observe and understand how they and people in general respond to incentives in their everyday lives. Teachers

can then use this understanding as a basis for emphasizing the economic content and conclusions underlying the activity in the lesson, and students are armed with tools for making rational decisions throughout their lives.

What is the essence of the economic way of thinking? What are the unique perspectives that economic analysis provides?

Economic reasoning is based on cost-benefit analysis. This analysis begins with a focus on costs. Every economic action involves a cost in time, effort and lost opportunities.

Economic reasoning assumes that people choose for good reasons and that they make choices by comparing the marginal or additional costs with the marginal or additional benefits of an action. Past or sunk costs are not relevant for the decision because these costs have already occurred and cannot be changed. This means that economic choices are not yes-or-no decisions but instead are more-or-less decisions. The economic perspective reminds us that we live in a world with more trade-offs than definite solutions.

Economic choices are driven by incentives. Changes in incentives influence behavior in predictable ways. Incentives are nothing more than changes in costs and benefits that in turn influence choices. The lessons in *Economics in Action* focus on these incentives. Supply and demand analysis is about incentives. Profits and business behavior are about incentives. Voluntary trade is about incentives.

Finally, economic actions create secondary effects. A poor analysis involves considering only the immediate and visible effects of a policy, while good economic analysis considers the secondary effects, which may not be immediately visible. Several lessons examine the secondary effects of government policies and market changes.

Economic Content
Along with teaching the economic way of thinking, the 14 lessons contained here

address a variety of economic concepts and content. In the United States, a coalition of economists and economic-education organizations, led by the National Council on Economic Education, reached a consensus about 20 important economic standards. NCEE published these standards and related benchmarks and applications in Voluntary National Content Standards in Economics (NCEE, 1997), which has greatly influenced the economics curriculum.

The 14 lessons in *Economics in Action* cover all 20 standards. To make it easy to relate the activities to economic content, each lesson also contains details about the content covered, a list of the concepts addressed, content-related materials such as overhead-transparency masters and handouts, and step-by-step procedures for addressing the content through discussions and group activities.

Is Activity-Based Economics Worthwhile?
Teachers sometimes express reservations about using active-learning methods in their classes because of the time these activities take. The activities in these lessons do take time: anywhere from about 10 to more than 45 minutes each. However, when used with appropriate and critically important preliminary and follow-up debriefing discussions, active learning can be a very efficient, as well as effective, way to teach economic content. Students are more likely to "get it" the first time, to remember what they learned and to enjoy the study of economics at the same time. Give activity-based economics a chance.

Jane S. Lopus
Professor of Economics
Director, Center for Economic Education
California State University, Hayward

John S. Morton
Vice President for Program Development
National Council on Economic Education

Content Standards: **What Should Be Taught In Economics and Why?**

One way to define the appropriate content of precollege economics is to develop a consensus about which ideas are most important for students to know. Standards are a guide schools may use to plan and teach what students should learn. Standards are statements of what we believe is important and why we believe it is important.

Because economics is one of the nine core subjects in the United States, the National Council on Economic Education led a coalition to develop Voluntary National Content Standards in Economics. The committee consisted of economists, university economic educators and teachers. The standards that follow are the result of their work. Although specifically developed for the United States, most of these standards reflect the core concepts in economics worldwide.

The lessons in *Economics in Action* provide some coverage of all 20 standards and are a good introduction to the core ideas in economics. These standards, a description of how students use the knowledge in the standards and a correlation of the standards to the *Economics in Action* lessons follow.

The Voluntary National Content Standards in Economics

1. Productive resources are limited. Therefore, people cannot have all the goods and services they want; as a result, they must choose some things and give up others.

    Students will be able to use this knowledge to identify what they gain and what they give up when they make choices.

2. Effective decision making requires comparing the additional costs of alternatives with the additional benefits. Most choices involve doing a little more or a little less of something; few choices are all-or-nothing decisions.

    Students will be able to use this knowledge to make effective decisions as consumers, producers, savers, investors, and citizens.

3. Different methods can be used to allocate goods and services. People, acting individually or collectively through government, must choose which methods to use to allocate different kinds of goods and services.

    Students will be able to use this knowledge to evaluate different methods of allocating goods and services by comparing the benefits and costs of each method.

4. People respond predictably to positive and negative incentives.

    Students will be able to use this knowledge to identify incentives that affect people's behavior and explain how incentives affect their own behavior.

5. Voluntary exchange occurs only when all participating parties expect to gain. This is true for trade among individuals or organizations within a nation, and among individuals or organizations in different nations.

    Students will be able to use this knowledge to negotiate exchanges and identify the gains to themselves and others. They will be able to compare the benefits and costs of policies that alter trade barriers between nations, such as tariffs and quotas.

6. When individuals, regions and nations specialize in what they can produce at the lowest cost and then trade with others, both production and consumption increase.

   Students will be able to use this knowledge to explain how they can benefit themselves and others by developing special skills and strengths.

7. Markets exist when buyers and sellers interact. This interaction determines market prices and thereby allocates scarce goods and services.

   Students will be able to use this knowledge to identify markets in which they have participated as a buyer and a seller and describe how the interaction of all buyers and sellers influences prices. They will also be able to predict how prices change when there is either a shortage or surplus of the product available.

8. Prices send signals and provide incentives to buyers and sellers. When supply or demand changes, market prices adjust, affecting incentives.

   Students will be able to use this knowledge to predict how prices change when the number of buyers or sellers in a market changes, and explain how the incentives facing individual buyers and sellers are affected.

9. Competition among sellers lowers costs and prices, and encourages producers to produce more of what consumers are willing and able to buy. Competition among buyers increases prices and allocates goods and services to those people who are willing and able to pay the most for them.

   Students will be able to use this knowledge to explain how changes in the level of competition in different markets can affect price and output levels.

10. Institutions evolve in market economies to help individuals and groups accomplish their goals. Banks, labor unions, corporations, legal systems and not-for-profit organizations are examples of important institutions. A different kind of institution, clearly defined and well enforced property rights, is essential to a market economy.

    Students will be able to use this knowledge to describe the roles of various economic institutions.

11. Money makes it easier to trade, borrow, save, invest and compare the value of goods and services.

    Students will be able to use this knowledge to explain how their lives would be more difficult in a world with no money or in a world where money sharply lost its value.

12. Interest rates, adjusted for inflation, rise and fall to balance the amount saved with the amount borrowed, thus affecting the allocation of scarce resources between present and future uses.

    Students will be able to use this knowledge to explain situations in which they pay or receive interest, and explain how they would react to changes in interest rates if they were making or receiving interest payments.

13. Income for most people is determined by the market value of the productive resources they sell. What workers earn depends, primarily, on the market value of what they produce and how productive they are.

    Students will be able to use this knowledge to predict future earnings based on their current plans for education, training and career options.

14. Entrepreneurs are people who take the risks of organizing productive resources to make goods and services. Profit is an important incentive that leads entrepreneurs to accept the risks of business failure.

    Students will be able to use this knowledge to identify the risks, returns and other characteristics of entrepreneurship that bear on its attractiveness as a career.

15. Investment in factories, machinery, new technology, and the health, education and training of people can raise future standards of living.

    Students will be able to use this knowledge to predict the consequences of investment decisions made by individuals, businesses and governments.

16. There is an economic role for government to play in a market economy whenever the benefits of a government policy outweigh its costs. Governments often provide for national defense, address environmental concerns, define and protect property rights, and attempt to make markets more competitive. Most government policies also redistribute income.

    Students will be able to use this knowledge to identify and evaluate the benefits and costs of alternative public policies, and assess who enjoys the benefits and who bears the costs.

17. Costs of government policies sometimes exceed benefits. This may occur because of incentives facing voters, government officials and government employees, because of actions by special interest groups that can impose costs on the general public, or because social goals other than economic efficiency are being pursued.

    Students will be able to use this knowledge to identify some public policies that may cost more than the benefits they generate,

    assess who enjoys the benefits and who bears the costs, and explain why the policies exist.

18. A nation's overall levels of income, employment and prices are determined by the interaction of spending and production decisions made by all households, firms, government agencies and others in the economy.

    Students will be able to use this knowledge to interpret media reports about current economic conditions and explain how these conditions can influence decisions made by consumers, producers and government policymakers.

19. Unemployment imposes costs on individuals and nations. Unexpected inflation imposes costs on many people and benefits some others because it arbitrarily redistributes purchasing power. Inflation can reduce the rate of growth of national living standards, because individuals and organizations use resources to protect themselves against the uncertainty of future prices.

    Students will be able to use this knowledge to make informed decisions by anticipating the consequences of inflation and unemployment.

20. Federal government budgetary policy and the Federal Reserve System's monetary policy influence the overall levels of employment, output and prices.

    Students will be able to use this knowledge to anticipate the impact of the federal government's and the Federal Reserve System's macroeconomic policy decisions on themselves and others.

A Correlation of the Lessons to the Voluntary National Content Standards in Economics

Standards	Lesson 1	Lesson 2	Lesson 3	Lesson 4	Lesson 5	Lesson 6	Lesson 7	Lesson 8	Lesson 9	Lesson 10	Lesson 11	Lesson 12	Lesson 13	Lesson 14
1. Scarcity		●	●						●					
2. Marginal costs/marginal benefits		●	●			●								
3. Allocation of goods and services		●	●											
4. Role of incentives	●		●	●	●									
5. Gains from trade	●												●	
6. Specialization and trade						●		●					●	
7. Markets; price and quantity determination							●			●				●
8. Role of price in market system							●							
9. Benefits of competition				●										
10. Role of economic institutions				●										
11. Role of money											●			●
12. Role of interest rates												●		
13. Role of resources in determining income								●						
14. Profit and the entrepreneur									●					
15. Growth								●						
16. Role of government						●				●				
17. Costs of government policies						●								
18. Circular flow-interdependence										●				
19. Unemployment and inflation											●			
20. Monetary and fiscal policy											●	●		

Taken from Voluntary National Content Standards in Economics, National Council on Economic Education, 1997.

Lesson 1 - Why People Trade

INTRODUCTION

Economics

Because students often take part in activities such as athletic competitions where one side wins and one side loses, they may not recognize that both sides win in *voluntary trade*. This is true because anyone who does not expect to gain from a trade would not voluntarily agree to do it. *Trade* is the exchange of goods and services. People decide to trade because they expect to benefit from it. When one or both parties cease to reap benefits from an exchange, or when they believe they can no longer gain from trading, exchanges stop. The idea that both sides benefit from voluntary trade is one of the most important concepts in economics and leads to the conclusion that, typically, the benefits of free trade far outweigh the costs. This idea applies to exchange among individuals and businesses as well as to trade among nations.

Reasoning

The economic way of thinking implies that people judge their satisfaction from a trade by weighing the expected benefits against the expected costs. Economic reasoning also tells us that different people place different *marginal values* on goods and services, making benefits from trade possible. With voluntary trade, both sides expect that the value of what they gain will be greater than the value of what they give up. The benefits of trade should become clear from this lesson: that is, voluntary exchange can make both individuals and nations better off.

CONCEPTS

Barriers to trade
Benefits of trade
Incentives
Trade
Voluntary exchange
(Optional) Utility

CONTENT STANDARDS

4. People respond predictably to positive and negative incentives.

5. Voluntary exchange occurs only when all participating parties expect to gain. This is true for trade among individuals or organizations within a nation, and among individuals or organizations in different nations.

OBJECTIVES

Students will
1. Participate in a trading activity and describe the incentives that encourage trade.

2. Explain the outcomes of voluntary trade.

3. Explain why there aren't any direct losers from voluntary trade.

LESSON DESCRIPTION

Students participate in a trading simulation and use this experience to discover the benefits of free trade. In a class discussion, they relate the simulation to concepts of regional versus universal trade, trade barriers and diminishing marginal value. They explain why both parties benefit from the trade.

TIME REQUIRED

45 minutes

MATERIALS

1. One brown paper bag for each student in the class

2. A large number of small items that are easy to exchange (miniature candy bars, small boxes of raisins, pencils, stickers, fruit, small boxes of juice, library passes). Before class, distribute the goods unequally in the bags; for instance, put only candy in some bags but give several items including candy to others. Give a few unlucky students only one or two less-popular items and give a few students an abundance of several different items such as candy, pencils and stickers. Try to create obvious contrasts among the contents of the bags.
    (Optional) Instead of preparing bags, ask students in advance to bring from home one or more small items to trade that they no longer want.

PROCEDURE

1. Discuss the following situation with the class: Imagine that Donna, a teenage driver, pulls up to a local gas station and puts $15 worth of gas in the tank. She then pays the station owner $15. Point out that this is an example of an exchange or a trade because $15 was traded for gas. Who gained and who lost in this situation? *One way of looking at this is that both people simultaneously gained something and lost or gave up something: The driver gave up $15 worth of purchasing power but gained several gallons of gasoline. The station owner gave up several gallons of gas but gained $15 in purchasing power.*
    Another way of looking at this is that both parties had overall, or net, gains. Both people likely feel better off because each now has something they value more than what they gave up: The teenager likely values the full tank of gas more than the $15, while the station owner likely values the $15 more than the gas. For each person,

the gains were greater than the losses. If this were not true, the teenager would have kept the money and the station owner would have kept the gas.

2. Tell students that in today's class they will participate in a trading activity. The purpose of the activity is to explore the reasons people, organizations and nations trade.

3. Ask the class, "Why do people trade?" Compile a list of answers on the board. Do not discourage any answers at this point. Explain that these responses represent hypotheses. Now the class must find evidence to support or reject these hypotheses.

4. Distribute to each student a bag with small items to trade. Assure students that they may keep whichever items they still possess at the end of the simulation. While students are still in their seats, have everyone privately examine the contents of their bags. Tell them not to show the contents to anyone.

TRADING ROUND 1

5. Divide the class in half. Announce that students will now have the opportunity to trade. Explain that they may trade any or all of the contents of their bags, but they may trade only with people on their side of the room. No one is required to participate in a trade. Allow five to 10 minutes for students to trade.

6. At the end of this first trading round, call students back together. Ask the following questions:
    A. How many students made a trade? *Responses will vary.*
    B. Ask everyone who made at least one trade to stand up. Why did they decide to trade? *Responses will vary but should point to the idea that the trades made them better off because they preferred*

what they got to what they gave up.

C. Ask for a show of hands: Of those who made trades, how many are better off as a result of the trades? *Generally, everyone who traded should be better off. Since trading was voluntary, if they did not expect to be better off, they should not have traded. This is the major point of this activity: Voluntary trade makes both parties who traded better off. Make sure this point is clear before going on.*

D. If anyone who traded said that he or she is not better off, ask him or her to explain why. *Sometimes students will say they thought they were trading for something better than what they actually got. Explain that this is a problem of poor information but not a problem of trading per se. Sometimes students will say they felt sorry for someone who didn't have as much as they did; so to help this person, they made a trade that caused them to be worse off. Explain that they probably feel better off as a result of helping others, so they have still gained. These situations do not contradict the point of the activity.*

E. Why did some students decide not to trade? *Responses will vary. Some students may say they were happy or satisfied with what they had and didn't want what others were willing to trade. This demonstrates that voluntary exchanges stop when both sides do not expect to gain. Some students will say they were not able to get what they wanted. However, everyone who does decide to trade is better off to some degree or they wouldn't have voluntarily traded.*

F. Did anyone trade more than once? Why? *Several students probably made numerous trades because they continued to become better off with each trade.*

G. Were any restrictions placed on trades? *Yes, students could trade only with people on their side of the room.*

H. How did this trade restriction affect trading decisions? *Many students will likely answer that they wanted to trade with someone in the other group. If anyone violated the rule that they could trade only with people on one side of the room, it points out a problem with trade barriers: When forces such as trade barriers interfere with people's incentives, there are incentives to violate the rules.*

TRADING ROUND 2

7. Announce that you will allow one more round of trading. This time there won't be any restrictions: Students may trade any item(s) with any other student(s) in the room if they choose to do so. Again, allow five to 10 minutes for trading.

8. Call students back together. Ask the following questions:

    A. How many students made a trade in this round? *Responses will vary, but you should find that students made more trades after the restrictions were removed.*

    B. How did the elimination of trade restrictions affect trading? *As trade was opened up, more students were able to find beneficial exchanges. This demonstrates the gains from free trade compared with restricted trade.*

    C. Did anyone make more than one trade? *Again, this number is likely to be larger than in the first round.*

    D. Why did you trade? *Answers will vary but should point to the fact that trade made them better off than before.*

    E. Of those who made trades, how many are better off as a result of the trades? *All students who traded should be better off from the trade if the trades were voluntary. Point out that those who traded in both Round 1 and Round 2 should be even better off after Round 2 trades.*

F. Identify some students who had a large number of the same item. Did anyone trade away some, but not all, of the item? *If this occurred, it is a demonstration of the law of diminishing marginal value (utility): The more you have of something, the less you value one more unit of it. For example, your tenth piece of candy is more easily given up than the only candy bar you possess; the marginal utility it provides is not as great as that of the first piece.*

G. Some people had more items – and more valuable items – to trade than others, just as with some countries. If you were one of the "poorer" students, were you able to trade? *Probably yes, unless some bags contained only items with no value to any student.*

H. Did any very poor students trade with any very "rich" students? *Probably yes. This demonstrates that people in wealthy nations aren't the only ones who benefit from trade and that mutually beneficial trade can take place between people in wealthy countries and poor countries.*

I. Was everyone totally happy with his or her trades? *Probably not, but emphasize that this is not the point. Students who had little to trade may not have been as pleased as those with a larger number of items. Some students may have traded merely to avoid feeling left out. Some students may not have been able to find something they were interested in at all. Students who traded and then realized they missed a better trade may have been unhappy. Finally, students who underestimated the costs of trade or overestimated its benefits – or both – may have been unhappy. Trading doesn't guarantee happiness. Economists merely maintain that trade will continue if people are better off after the trade than if they had not traded at all.*

J. Did your trading behavior support or disprove the class's hypotheses about why people trade? *Answers will vary. Refer to the hypotheses on the board and compare them with the reasons students gave for trading.*

K. What conclusions can you draw from this simulation? *Again, answers will vary but should include some mention of the gains from trade and the concept that both sides benefit and no one loses.*

9.   **(Optional)** Here is an alternative way to conduct the trading activity that uses numbers to show gains from trade. Distribute the bags with the trading items to students as before. Ask students to rate, on a scale of one to five, their satisfaction with their bag's contents, with five being very satisfied and one being dissatisfied. Instruct students to write the number on the bag. Explain that economists use the term *utility* to describe the satisfaction people receive from things – in this case, the contents of their bag. Ask for a show of hands and count how many students rated their utility at 5, 4, 3, 2 and 1, and keep a tally on the board.

After the Round 1 trading session, ask students to rate their satisfaction with the items they now have and to again record their satisfaction by writing a number from one to five on their bag. Survey the class regarding their utility and record the responses on the board. The numbers should be higher than before trading, demonstrating the benefits from trade.

After the Round 2 trading session, ask students to rate their satisfaction with the items they now have and to again record the number on their bag. Survey the class again regarding their utility and write the numbers on the board. Students who traded should rank their utility higher than they did in the first round of trading. Students should also note that the overall utility rankings for the class have increased with each trading round.

CLOSURE

Summarize the lesson by having students discuss how the trading sessions resembled trading in the real world. Some differences are obvious: Students didn't exchange money and they didn't have to work – i.e., incur production costs – to get the items they traded. Compare this session with the gasoline scenario from the beginning of the lesson and notice the many similarities. You may wish to point out that an idea underlying free trade is that different people place different marginal values on items. People tend to give up items they value less than the item they are getting in exchange. In this way, students ended the activity with an item they valued more than the one they had when trading began.

Lesson 2 - Economic Decision Making

INTRODUCTION

Economics

In everyday life, people engage in *economizing behavior*. Whether consciously or unconsciously, they weigh the relative costs and benefits of each alternative when faced with a choice and then choose the one that provides them with the greatest anticipated benefits. While some decisions are obviously more important than others, the study of economics emphasizes that no decision is cost-free. Economists consider the real cost, or *opportunity cost*, of any decision to be the best alternative not chosen. This lesson introduces students to a five-step decision-making model that provides a framework for making rational choices about issues affecting their everyday lives as well as broader social issues.

Reasoning

Economic reasoning is an analysis of costs and benefits to make rational choices. However, different people have different values and may make different decisions while using the same criteria. Students discover this while working with two basic economic premises: People economize and people respond to incentives in predictable ways. Students are encouraged to weigh the costs and benefits of alternatives and to identify the real cost, or opportunity cost, of a decision.

CONCEPTS

Allocation
Choices
Economic systems
Economizing behavior
Opportunity cost
Scarcity

CONTENT STANDARDS

1. Productive resources are limited. Therefore, people cannot have all the goods and services they want; as a result, they must choose some things and give up others.

2. Effective decision making requires comparing the additional costs of alternatives with the additional benefits. Most choices involve doing a little more or a little less of something; few choices are all-or-nothing decisions.

3. Different methods can be used to allocate goods and services. People, acting individually or collectively through government, must choose which methods to use to allocate different kinds of goods and services.

OBJECTIVES

Students will
1. List and apply the steps of an economic decision-making model.

2. Classify economic activity into three major categories of economic systems: market, tradition and command.

LESSON DESCRIPTION

Students brainstorm ways to allocate a scarce good within the classroom. Then they work with a decision-making model that helps them make a decision about this allocation by showing them how to evaluate the merits of each alternative. Finally, students classify examples of market, traditional and command economic systems.

TIME REQUIRED

45 minutes for the decision-making activity and 20 minutes for the economic-systems activity.

MATERIALS

1. Visuals 2.1, 2.2 and 2.3

2. A copy of Activity 2.1 for each student

3. Identical desirable items such as a candy bar, homework pass or extra-credit points for small groups to allocate to one student in each group. It is best if the items cannot be divided into parts.

PROCEDURE

DECISION-MAKING ACTIVITY

1. Arrange students in groups of three to four. Display a desirable item such as a coupon for five extra-credit points, a candy bar or a homework pass. Ask the class how many students would like to have this item today. Assure them that you are more than willing to give them the item and that indeed one student in each group will leave class today with the item in hand; this is not a trick question.

2. Explain to students that the items in your possession are scarce because they are both limited *and* desired by the students in the class. Tell them scarcity is a condition we face in every aspect of our economic lives. Both individuals and societies must devise ways to deal with this problem of scarcity. Suggest that this is exactly what they will be doing in this lesson. Assure them that you have only a limited number of each item to allocate today, one per group; there are no more, for example, hiding behind your desk. Ask "How will I determine who among you will receive this?" Instruct the groups to generate a list of all the different ways they can think of for you to determine who gets the item in their group. Do not discourage any answers!

3. Give students about five minutes to brainstorm.

4. Create a list of suggestions on the board by eliciting responses from each group. Again, it is very important not to discourage any answers. Depending on the item to be allocated, students may suggest alternatives such as giving it to the student with the highest or lowest grade, the student who is hungriest or the student willing to pay the most. They may also suggest using a lottery to decide.

5. Explain that economics stresses the importance of people making decisions in a careful way. This allows people to know what they are giving up when they choose among alternatives. The best alternative that you give up when you make a decision is called the *opportunity cost*. Suggest that economics can provide a great way to help the groups decide how to allocate their good. Display Visual 2.1, "The PACED Decision-Making Model." Go over each of the five steps.

6. Distribute a copy of Activity 2.1 to each student. Now that the class has helped you create a list of possible allocation methods on the board, tell students that they will use the PACED model to determine who will really get the good in their group. Display Visual 2.2 and begin the PACED process as a class. Ask:
    A. What is the problem? *Deciding who will get the one good in each group*
    B. What are the alternatives? *Everything the class suggested that you listed on the board*

7. To streamline the PACED process, ask each group to select the five alternatives from the class list that they believe to be the best. They should list these five alternatives in the space provided on Activity 2.1. You may want to ask for a selection of the five alternatives to write on Visual 2.2 as well.

8. Ask "What criteria are important to you in making this decision?" *Answers will vary, but may include things such as fairness, equality, need and willingness to pay.* Write a sampling of the responses in the space provided on Visual 2.2. Ask each group to decide which four criteria they deem most important. Have each group list these criteria at the top of their decision-making grids. Ask "How should these criteria be ranked?" Have them rank order the criteria on their grids by giving a score of 1 to their top criterion, 2 to their next most important and so on.

9. Now ask students how they should evaluate the alternatives. It may be useful to go through the evaluation process for one alternative using the overhead with the whole class. If the group decides that an alternative successfully meets a criterion, they should put a plus (+) in the appropriate square on their grid. If they feel an alternative does not meet a certain criterion, they should write a minus (-) in that box. If groups are unsure whether an alternative meets the criterion, they should put a question mark in that box. Once you have completed an example on the overhead, instruct the groups to evaluate each of their five alternatives on the basis of each of their four criteria.

10. Once all groups have filled in their grids, tell the class that it is time to make a decision. Each group should do this by calculating the net value (number of pluses less number of minuses) of each alternative in their grid. The alternative with the highest positive net value will probably be the group's decision, unless they feel stronger about the ranking of the various criteria than they do about the net value. Have each group allocate the item to the person they chose through their decision-making process.

11. Ask groups to explain who got the good and how the decision was made. As the groups report, encourage them to explain which criteria were important to them in making their final decision. For example, one group may have selected fairness as their most important criterion, while another group may have thought that who wanted it most was the most important. Make a list on the board of the allocation methods used by each group.

ECONOMIC-SYSTEMS ACTIVITY

12. Explain to students that there are different ways of classifying economic activities. Each type of economic system represents a different set of rules for economic behavior. Knowing the different classifications will help students recognize differing forms of economic activity in both our economy and the decisions they have just made about how to allocate the good in their group. Point out to students that societies often have similar decisions to make regarding goods and services such as health care, environmental quality, education and housing.

13. Display Visual 2.3, "Economic Systems." Explain the characteristics of each type of system.

14. Either as a class or in small groups, have students categorize the group-allocation decisions they made by the type of system their process most closely resembles. For example, if any groups decided to sell the item to the student willing to pay the most, this would be representative of a market economy. If a group let one person make the decision for them, this is representative of a command system. Some decisions, such as a lottery or deciding to give the item to the tallest person in the group, may not fall clearly into any of the categories. These decisions may resemble traditional systems if they are based on the way things have been done in the past.

CLOSURE

Point out that the PACED model is a very useful tool they can use to make decisions about
important issues affecting society and about
personal problems that affect their own lives.
Personal problems include what to do with
spare time on the weekend, which movie to
see, which part-time job to take or where to go
to dinner before the prom. Social problems
include issues such as which immigration policy a nation should adopt, whether a city
should raise its property taxes, whether a
school district should build a new high school
or what the legal minimum drinking age
should be.

Have the class select a current economic issue
of interest to them. Assign groups to use the
PACED model to make a decision about the
issue. Compare and discuss the groups' results
and review the steps of the economic decision-
making process.

VISUAL 2.1
THE PACED DECISION-MAKING MODEL

P. What is the **PROBLEM**?
- What decision are you trying to make?
- What is the issue at hand?

A. What are the **ALTERNATIVES**?
- What actions are you considering?
- What options are available to you in this decision?

C. What are the **CRITERIA** important to the decision?
- What goals do you hope to accomplish in making your decision?
- What characteristics are you looking for in your result?
- Which criteria are more important than others? How do you rank them?

E. **EVALUATE** each alternative.
- Evaluate each alternative on the basis of each criterion.
- Give each alternative a plus (+) or a minus (–) according to how well it meets each criterion.

D. Make a **DECISION**.
- Calculate the net value of each alternative; which alternative best meets your highest-ranking criteria?
- What do you gain with each alternative?
- What do you give up with each alternative?

VISUAL 2.2
PACED DECISION-MAKING GRID

P. What is the **problem**?
A. What are the **alternatives**?
C. What are the **criteria**?
E. Evaluate the alternatives.
D. Make a **decision**.

	Criterion	Criterion	Criterion	Criterion
	Ranking	Ranking	Ranking	Ranking
Alternative				
Alternative				
Alternative				
Alternative				
Alternative				

ECONOMICS IN ACTION, © NATIONAL COUNCIL ON ECONOMIC EDUCATION, NEW YORK, N.Y.

VISUAL 2.3
ECONOMIC SYSTEMS

TRADITIONAL ECONOMIES
Decisions about what to produce, how to produce and to whom goods and services will be allocated generally repeat decisions made in earlier times or by previous generations. Continuity and stability are valued in economic life.

MARKET ECONOMIES
Individuals and businesses own productive resources and make the decisions about what to produce, how to produce and to whom goods and services will be allocated. The market prices that result from individual and business decisions act as signals to producers, telling them what buyers want. Goods and services are allocated on the basis of prices.

COMMAND ECONOMIES
An authority such as a feudal lord, a government agency or central planners decide what to produce, how to produce and to whom goods and services will be allocated.

ACTIVITY 2.1
PACED DECISION-MAKING GRID

P. What is the **problem**?
A. What are the **alternatives**?
C. What are the **criteria**?
E. Evaluate the alternatives.
D. Make a **decision**.

	Criterion Ranking	Criterion Ranking	Criterion Ranking	Criterion Ranking
Alternative				
Alternative				
Alternative				
Alternative				
Alternative				

Lesson 3 - Using Economic Reasoning To Solve Mysteries

INTRODUCTION

Economics

Perhaps the simplest definition of the social science of economics is the study of *choice*. Economics takes as its starting point certain assumptions largely centered on the problem of *scarcity*, or the imbalance of our unlimited wants in the face of limited resources. An economist will approach any situation with these assumptions in mind. Economists also assume that people are *utility-maximizing* creatures or, more simply, that they constantly strive to satisfy their desires. In this quest, people encounter limits, necessitating choices. All choices involve costs. Economists also examine the economic systems people work within, because these systems determine the rules of the game to which people are subject.

Reasoning

Economic theory suggests that we are faced with choices nearly every moment of every day. In fact, even when we believe we do not have a choice, an economist would insist that we do. The "Guide to Economic Thinking" boils down the essential assumptions of economic reasoning into a format students can easily comprehend. The guide is a tool that can help them make sense of choices and incentives. Economic reasoning lends itself to posing questions in the form of mysteries. Initially, students often find many fundamental tenets of economics to be counterintuitive. As they examine more and more mysteries, they begin to "think like an economist" and what once seemed at odds with ordinary experience and judgment becomes clear.

CONCEPTS

Choice
Economic reasoning
Incentives
Opportunity cost

CONTENT STANDARDS

1. Productive resources are limited. Therefore, people cannot have all the goods and services they want; as a result, they must choose some things and give up others.

2. Effective decision making requires comparing the additional costs of alternatives with the additional benefits. Most choices involve doing a little more or a little less of something; few choices are all-or-nothing decisions.

3. Different methods can be used to allocate goods and services. People, acting individually or collectively through government, must choose which methods to use to allocate different kinds of goods and services.

4. People respond predictably to positive and negative incentives.

OBJECTIVES

Students will
1. Distinguish between relevant and irrelevant information.

2. Use relevant clues to help identify the economic principles useful in solving an economic mystery.

3. Use the principles of economics, as laid out in the "Guide to Economic Thinking," to solve the economic mystery.

LESSON DESCRIPTION

Students ponder an economic mystery: Why do professional athletes, many of whom never finish college, earn far higher salaries than people who perform worthy services such as teachers and firefighters? The students discuss various explanations for this seemingly non-sensical inequity and then examine a set of clues and the principles of economic reasoning to help them arrive at a solution for the mystery.

TIME REQUIRED

45 minutes

MATERIALS

1. Visuals 3.1 and 3.2

2. One copy of Activity 3.1, "Mystery Clues," for each group of students, cut out and assembled as a set of cards, with each card containing one clue

PROCEDURE

1. Explain to students that the purpose of this lesson is to help them think like economists. Specifically, they will sharpen and use their economic-reasoning skills by using economic principles and clues to solve an economic mystery about some things near and dear to them: sports and money.

2. Display Visual 3.1, "The Guide to Economic Thinking." Go over each of the principles with the class.

3. Display Visual 3.2, "Why Adults Are Paid Big Bucks to Play Games." Read through the scenario that sets up the mystery, and tell the students that the actual mystery is the question in italics. Invite them to speculate on the solution. Suggest that "The Guide to Economic Thinking" reappears at the bottom of the visual for good reason: It can help them find a solution.

4. Divide the class into groups of three to four students. Ask each group to select a discussion leader and a reporter. Give each group a set of clues (the cards you created using Activity 3.1). Put each group to work with the following directions:

A. Their task is to propose a solution to the mystery and explain their solution by using economic reasoning. They should apply the principles in "The Guide to Economic Thinking."

B. Assure the students that each group has the same set of clues and all information provided in these clues is true; there is no false information included. However, some of the clues will be useful or relevant in solving the mystery, and some will not. Students therefore should not get bogged down in arguing the truthfulness of the clues themselves but rather should spend their time determining if the information contained in a particular clue will help them solve the mystery. Tell the students there is no significance to the numbers on the clues; the numbers simply provide an easy way to refer to each clue.

C. Tell the groups to lay their clue cards out in the shape of a pyramid, though not necessarily a perfectly symmetrical one. Clues the group deems irrelevant should form the base of the pyramid. The clue they believe is the most important should be the apex. Clues that are relevant but of secondary importance to the apex clue should form the middle layer(s) of the pyramid. Do not give the students a number of layers for their pyramids; encourage them to rank the importance of their clues in the best way they see fit. Tell the students to keep "The Guide to Economic Thinking" in mind as they work on the problem. In addition to sorting their clues, they should determine which principles of the guide were most relevant as they developed their solution to the mystery. Tell them they will report their solution to the class and should include an explanation of how this principle helped them sort the clues and reach their conclusion.

D. Give the students five to 10 minutes to complete their discussions and construct their pyramids. At the end of this discussion period, the reporter should be ready to explain his or her group's solution and pyramid to the rest of the class.

5. Monitor the groups' discussions. You'll probably find some disagreement in many groups. This is to be expected and not necessarily discouraged. You may also find that students are reluctant to declare any of the clues irrelevant, often using convoluted logic to plead the case of a particular clue. Remind them that an important objective of this lesson is being able to sort out the relevant information from the useless: Not all information is of equal value.

6. Ask each reporter to share the group's solution with the class and to justify its choice of the relevant clues and principles of economic reasoning. *Clues 2 and 5 are the most important for solving the mystery. The supply of extremely talented athletes is small, yet the demand to view athletes' performances is very great. This combination results in high salaries relative to people in other professions. Students will probably identify Principles 1, 2 and 3 from the guide as the most relevant in solving the mystery, although arguments could be made for all of the principles. Fans willingly choose to pay high prices for game tickets (Principle 1). Talented players choose to give up college educations to go pro, because the opportunity cost of staying in college is a very high salary (Principles 1, 2 and 3).*

CLOSURE

Review the main points of the lesson. Revisit each of the principles of the guide with the students.

For a follow-up assignment, ask the students to look for newspaper articles that include economic mysteries. Choose the best articles and distribute them to the class. Have the students summarize the articles and describe which principles from "The Guide to Economic Thinking" apply to the stories and help them solve the mystery.

OPTIONAL EXTENSION

Economic mysteries can be a fun and useful theme throughout your course. Here are some examples of other mysteries that have been used successfully with high school classes:

1. Young people are the future of our country. Why is the level of unemployment highest among young people?

2. American consumers are cost-conscious. Why do they buy brand-name products when they could save money buying store brands that are just as good?

3. U.S. autoworkers have fewer jobs because not enough people buy American cars. Why do Americans buy foreign cars?

WRITING YOUR OWN MYSTERY

Writing and using new mysteries is a good way to continue to emphasize "The Guide to Economic Thinking," whether the mysteries are written by the teacher or by students. If you are interested in writing your own mysteries, follow these simple steps:

1. **Be on the lookout for things that seem odd.** Pay attention to the news, which is where most economic mysteries originate. Look for discrepancies between a reported event and your own sense of what ought to be expected under the circumstances. Discrepancies invite explanation; they provide excellent focal points for exercises in economic reasoning. (For example, athletes are playing games, so why are they paid more than nurses who save lives?)

2. **Develop a primary proposition.** Once you have noticed a problem, describe one side of it in a straightforward manner. This proposition should state something that is generally known or that looks reasonable on its face. (For example, many professional athletes never finish college.)

3. **Develop an opposing proposition.** If you're onto a good mystery, the facts of the case will suggest information that runs counter to the primary proposition. State them in an opposing proposition, thus implying a mystery or area of uncertainty

that begs explaining. In thinking about opposing propositions, you might find it helpful to notice that they often begin with "yet," "but" or "however." (For example, annual salaries for professional athletes are much higher than salaries for teachers, yet teachers have college educations and perform valuable services to society by helping educate others.)

4. **Identify the mystery explicitly.** While the juxtaposition of the two main propositions is likely to suggest what the mystery is, you should nonetheless identify the mystery explicitly. (For example, "Why are grown men and women paid millions of dollars to play games?")

5. **Make sure that all your clues are true and that some are irrelevant to the mystery.** It is easy to feel overwhelmed with data in these days of near-instant access to ubiquitous media. And just because a fact is true doesn't mean it has value: Think about the diversions that "facts" provide on TV crime shows. Help students learn to distinguish between relevant and irrelevant facts by writing six to 10 clues that are straightforward, unbiased statements, but make sure at least a few don't relate directly to the mystery. (For example, coaches may encourage competition among their players as a way to spark peak performance, but this doesn't help students explain why some athletes make more money than firefighters.)

6. **Focus on economic principles in trying to explain the mystery.** Emphasizing the principles of "The Guide to Economic Thinking" will maintain your economic focus. These principles highlight, for example, the importance of getting the incentives straight in any analysis of an economic mystery. In fact, nearly all economic mysteries can be resolved or clarified in large measure by attention to incentives.

VISUAL 3.1
THE GUIDE TO ECONOMIC THINKING

1. **People *choose*.**
   Most situations involve making choices. People evaluate the costs and benefits of different alternatives and choose the alternative that seems best to them.

2. **People's choices involve *costs*.**
   Costs do not necessarily involve money. The most important type of cost is *opportunity cost*: the next best alternative that people give up when they make a choice.

3. **People respond to *incentives* in predictable ways.**
   Incentives are actions or rewards that encourage people to act in a certain way. Incentives can be either positive or negative. When incentives change, people's behavior changes in predictable ways.

4. **People create *economic systems* that influence individual choices and incentives.**
   How people cooperate is governed by written and unwritten rules. As the rules change, incentives – and consequently people's behaviors – change.

5. **People gain when they *trade* voluntarily.**
   People can produce goods and services at lower opportunity costs when they specialize in what they do best. Then they can trade what they produce for goods or services that would be more costly for them to produce. In this way, both sides gain.

6. **People's choices have consequences that lie in the *future*.**
   The important costs and benefits in economic decision making are those that will appear in the future. The study of economics stresses the importance of making decisions about the future because we can influence only the future; we cannot influence things that happened in the past.

VISUAL 3.2
WHY ADULTS ARE PAID BIG BUCKS TO PLAY GAMES

THE MYSTERY

Many professional athletes never finish college. Some go directly into professional sports from high school. Yet professional athletes are frequently paid salaries totaling millions of dollars a year. Annual salaries for professional football players range from a few hundred thousand dollars to several million dollars. The story is much the same among professional athletes in basketball and baseball.

Yet other people who perform worthy services – nurses, police officers, firefighters and teachers – receive salaries far short of the amounts paid to professional athletes. What is wrong with our values?

Why are grown men and women paid salaries totaling millions of dollars to play games?

The Guide to Economic Thinking

1. People *choose*.

2. People's choices involve *costs*.

3. People respond to *incentives* in predictable ways.

4. People create *economic systems* that influence individual choices and incentives.

5. People gain when they *trade* voluntarily.

6. People's choices have consequences that lie in the *future*.

ACTIVITY 3.1
MYSTERY CLUES

1. In addition to salaries from playing games, athletes often earn money through endorsements, speaking engagements, signing autographs and other nongame activities.	**2.** Few people possess the skills required to throw big-league fast balls, deliver one-handed jams and toss game-winning touchdown passes.
3. Many professional athletes have gone to college.	**4.** Coaches encourage competition among their players as a way to bring out their best performance.
5. Fans will pay to see professional athletes perform in person; they also tune in by the millions to watch athletes on television.	**6.** When professional players strike, this is a turn-off for many fans.
7. Like police officers and firefighters, professional athletes risk serious injury.	**8.** The nonlabor costs of running a team such as uniforms, equipment and airfares have been increasing recently.
9. Famous athletes regularly appear on the covers of popular magazines.	**10.** Some athletes return to college and complete their education after they retire from sports.

Lesson 4 - Property Rights in a Market Economy

INTRODUCTION

Economics

All *market economies* have several basic characteristics in common including private property, free enterprise, self-interest, competition, a price system and limited (laissez-faire) government. *Property rights*, defined as individual ownership and control of resources and products, are the fundamental characteristic of a market system. Property rights affect the way markets allocate resources.

If property rights are well defined and enforced and markets are competitive, a market system ensures that resources are used in their most valued manner. Private ownership encourages people to take good care of property. It also encourages productive development of property and conservation of resources for the future. This is the beauty of a market economy.

But the "if" is a big one, and, unfortunately, property rights to many natural resources are poorly defined. When property rights are not clearly defined, resources may be wasted or used inefficiently. Therefore, an important role for government in a market economy is to try to ensure that property rights are clearly defined and protected.

Reasoning

Economic reasoning says that people respond to incentives and that the consequences of actions lie in the future. When property rights are not clearly defined, people acting in their own self-interest may respond to incentives that are counter to the long-run objectives of society. Environmental pollution provides many examples of this phenomenon. When students understand this idea, they can then understand the importance of defining and enforcing property rights.

CONCEPTS

Competition
Free enterprise
Limited government
Private property (property rights)
Self-interest
System of markets and prices

CONTENT STANDARDS

4. People respond predictably to positive and negative incentives.

9. Competition among sellers lowers costs and prices, and encourages producers to produce more of what consumers are willing and able to buy. Competition among buyers increases prices and allocates goods and services to those people who are willing and able to pay the most for them.

10. Institutions evolve in market economies to help individuals and groups accomplish their goals. Banks, labor unions, corporations, legal systems and not-for-profit organizations are examples of important institutions. A different kind of institution, clearly defined and well enforced property rights, is essential to a market economy.

OBJECTIVES

Students will
1. Analyze the basic characteristics of a market economy.

2. Participate in or observe an activity demonstrating how property rights affect behavior.

3. Compare resource use when property rights are clearly defined with resource use when property rights are not clearly defined.

LESSON DESCRIPTION

Students discuss private property, free enterprise, self-interest, competition, a system of markets and prices, and limited government as characteristics of market economies. They participate in or observe an activity demonstrating that property rights affect incentives and behavior. They conclude that it is important to have clearly defined property rights so resources are not wasted.

TIME REQUIRED

60 minutes

MATERIALS

1. Visual 4.1

2. 50 paper clips

3. One bag of small candy (or other desirable items such as pennies or extra-credit points) for Round 1 and one bag for Round 2. To be safe, you need 100 items for each round.

4. A roll of masking tape (or a ball of string or yarn)

PROCEDURE

1. Ask students what they believe makes a market economy (also called a *capitalist system*, a *free-market system*, or a *free-enterprise system*) different from the economic system in Cuba or in the former Soviet Union. Write suggested answers on the board.

2. Display Visual 4.1, "Basic Characteristics of a Market Economy." Tell students that many economists list these characteristics when describing a pure market system. Remind students that although the United States is predominantly a free-market system, all countries have mixed systems to some extent; no economy is purely market, command or traditional. (For an explanation of all these economic systems, see Visual 2.3.) Discuss the characteristics of market systems listed on Visual 4.1.

A. Private Property. A system of private property means that individuals and private businesses, not the government, own most land and capital goods. The right to own private property (property rights) provides incentives to owners to take care of the property and to invest in it and therefore encourages the efficient allocation of resources and economic growth.

B. Free Enterprise. Free enterprise means that, within legal limits, individuals are free to open businesses and to produce and sell the goods and services of their choice. Individuals are also free to work where they want and to buy the goods and services they want with their earnings.

C. Self-Interest. Self-interest drives people to get the best job they can, to get the most for their money and to earn the most profit in their businesses. When everyone does this, resources are used to produce the goods and services everyone wants, which is a desirable outcome. Self-interest is not the same as selfishness and does not mean that people cannot and do not help others. As Adam Smith pointed out in 1776 in his book *The Wealth of Nations*, people acting in their own self-interest are guided as if by an "invisible hand" to do what is best for society as a whole.

D. Competition. Competition keeps prices in line with the costs of production. If one seller raises prices in an attempt to earn excessive profits, competition from other sellers (who also want to earn profits) will drive the prices down. Pure competition assumes that sellers can easily leave one business and easily enter another one. Competition among buyers prevents any one buyer from controlling prices by refusing to buy something.

E. System of Markets and Prices. Markets bring together buyers and sellers of goods and services. In a market system, the forces of supply and demand, not the government, determine prices. If there is a surplus of goods available at the going price, the price will fall. If there is a shortage of goods available at the going price, the price will rise.

F. Limited Government. Although market economies can operate in most respects without government interference, there are important roles for government to play. At a minimum, government is needed to define and enforce property rights and to provide some goods and services such as national defense that are not provided efficiently by markets. (For an explanation of public goods, see Lesson 5.)

3. Tell the students they will participate in or observe a short activity that focuses on one or more of the characteristics of a market economy. Clear an area in the center of the room at least six feet in diameter with room for students to stand around it. Ask for 10 volunteers for a well-paying job. Display a bag of candy representing the pay.

ROUND 1

4. Ask the 10 volunteers to stand in a circle around the cleared area. Scatter 50 paper clips inside the circle. Tell the students they will be paid to pick up the paper clips. There will be two time periods, each lasting 30 seconds. If they decide to pick up any paper clips during the first 30 seconds, they will be paid one piece of candy for each paper clip. If they decide to pick up paper clips during the second 30 seconds, they will be paid *two* pieces of candy for each paper clip. Students must turn in all the paper clips they pick up at the end of each period. Appoint a student to help distribute the candy in exchange for the paper clips when the time comes, and appoint a student timekeeper to say "Stop!" when 30 seconds are up.

You may want to tell students at this point that the paper clips represent a natural resource such as fish or trees or whales. In the first time period, the fish are smaller and less valuable to society, so the payoff is smaller. In the second period,

the fish are larger and more valuable to society, so the payoff is higher.

A. Begin the first 30-second time period. The student volunteers may talk among themselves about waiting until the second 30 seconds to pick up the clips for the higher payoff, but it is likely that soon someone will start gathering the clips as fast as he or she can, and others will also jump in to pick up the clips. Probably all the clips will be picked up early in the first 30 seconds.

B. Pay the students one candy for each clip they picked up.

C. Run the second 30-second time period even if students picked up all the clips during the first 30 seconds.

D. Pay the students two candies for any clips they picked up in the second period. Make sure you have all 50 paper clips.

ROUND 2

5. Use four long strips of masking tape (or string or yarn depending on the floor) to line the cleared area of the floor in a tic-tac-toe pattern.

Have one student stand in each square, and have the tenth student stand off to the side. Tell the tenth student you are sorry, but in this round not everyone will have the right to collect or fish for the paper clips. Later you can point out that everyone may not be able to own property.

Scatter the 50 paper clips so they fall into the various cells. Make sure a few of the clips lie on the tape so it is not clear which cell they are in.

Tell the students you are going to repeat the game, again paying one candy for each clip they pick up in the first 30 seconds and two candies for each clip they pick up in the second 30 seconds. However, this time people may pick up only the clips in their own cell. Students will probably ask who can pick up the clips that are on the taped lines between the cells. Just shrug in response.

A. Begin the first 30-second time period. This time, students will probably decide to wait until the second 30 seconds to pick up the clips with the possible exception of the ones on the boundaries. Because they have property rights over their cell – no one else can pick up their clips – they have the incentive to wait for the higher payoff. This reflects the higher value society places on the resource.

B. If any students pick up the clips during the first 30-second period, pay them one candy when the time is up.

C. Begin the second 30-second period. Students will probably pick up most of the clips during this period. Pay the students two candies for each paper clip.

6. Discuss the activity by asking the following questions:

A. Why did people have incentives in Round 1 to pick up the clips during the first 30 seconds even though the payoff was higher if they waited? *If they waited until the second 30 seconds, no clips would have been left: Others, acting in their self-interest, would have already picked them up.*

B. Why did people have incentives in Round 2 to pick up the clips during the second 30 seconds? How were incentives different in Round 2? *In the second round, students could pick up only the clips in his or her cell, so everyone had incentives to wait for the higher payoff, reflecting the higher value society placed on the resource in the second 30 seconds. The resources were private property, which provided incentives to the owners to use them in the best way.*

C. What did students do in Round 2 about the paper clips that fell on the boundaries? *Answers will vary. It is likely that students picked up the clips that fell on the boundaries during the first 30 seconds, since if they didn't, someone else would have. This is equivalent to what happened in Round 1. If students asked you what to do about clips on the boundaries earlier, they were pointing out that the* property rights to these clips were not clearly defined; and they were asking you, the authority, to define who had the property rights. This emphasizes the need for laws to decide who has property rights when such rights are not clearly defined.

D. If any students in Round 2 picked up the clips in the first 30 seconds (other than the clips on the boundaries), ask them why they did so, since they would have had higher pay had they waited. *Sometimes a few students will say they didn't believe you would really pay them more in the second 30 seconds. This provides an opportunity to discuss the importance of knowing that property rights will be enforced – either by you in the game or by the government in real life.*

E. Imagine that the paper clips were whales, the floor was the ocean and the student volunteers were whale hunters. How can the activity relate to problems of harvesting whales? *In Round 1, when no one had clear property rights, no one had the incentive or right to maintain or control the stock of whales since they couldn't stop others from harvesting them. In Round 2, people had clearly defined property rights to the whales, so there were incentives to manage and control the whale population: in other words, to pick up the clips during the second 30 seconds.*

F. Remind students that there is concern about whales becoming extinct, and there are campaigns to "Save the Whales." Ask students to think for a minute about the amount of beef and chicken consumed every day. Why aren't cattle and chickens in danger of extinction, along with whales? *Cattle and chicken are privately owned and raised on private property. Ranchers have incentives to raise them and sell them when they bring in the best prices and are most highly valued by society. Ranchers have incentives to maintain their stocks of cattle and chicken, and they* *are able to do so because the cattle and chicken are privately owned. On the other hand, property rights to the ocean are in most cases not clearly defined; so whale hunters have incentives to hunt the whales whenever they can, regardless of the future costs and benefits to society.*

G. Ask students to think of other resources for which property rights are not clearly defined. What problems occur as a result? *In many cases, property rights to air and water are not clearly defined. Environmental pollution often occurs in these situations because, in the absence of laws imposed by government, many people and businesses do not have incentives to keep the resources clean, and resources may be abused or overused. To emphasize this point, ask students which is more likely to be polluted: a privately owned lake or a public lake? Noise pollution is another example involving a lack of clearly defined property rights.*

7. **(Optional)** Here are other ideas for conducting this activity.

    A. To involve the entire class in the activity directly, students who are picking up the paper clips may choose one or two partners who remain outside the circle so each of the 10 volunteers represents a team of two or three students.

    B. You may conduct the activity using an overhead projector, in which case students stand around it and you scatter paper clips on the screen. Use a marker and transparency to divide the screen for Round 2.

    C. It may be worthwhile to run Round 1 a second time before running Round 2. Students tend to have even less regard for the "environment" in Round 1 the second time, once they witness how their classmates respond to the incentives.

    D. If unexpected outcomes occur in the activity, these often involve property rights. For example, in Round 1 a student

may try to hide paper clips during the first 30 seconds and turn them in for higher pay during the second 30 seconds. The student is demonstrating that he or she has the incentive to break the rules in order to assert property rights over the clips.

CLOSURE

Review and emphasize the major points of the paper-clip activity and relate the activity back to the concepts on Visual 4.1. The activity demonstrates that people have different incentives when property rights are clearly defined (Round 2) compared with when such rights are not clearly spelled out (Round 1). The activity demonstrates the importance of private-property rights in order for resources to be used in the manner most valued by society. People have incentives to act in their self-interest, which usually works to society's benefit. However, when property rights are not clearly defined (as is frequently the case with natural resources), there is often a role for government to pass laws that decide who has the right to the property or for government to get involved in other ways.

VISUAL 4.1
BASIC CHARACTERISTICS OF A MARKET ECONOMY

A. Private Property

B. Free Enterprise

C. Self-Interest

D. Competition

E. System of Markets and Prices

F. Limited Government

Lesson 5 - The Role of Government In a Market Economy

INTRODUCTION

Economics

Governments play limited roles in market economies because most goods and services can be freely and efficiently produced in the private sector. However, in cases referred to as *market failures*, unregulated markets result in the systematic underproduction or overproduction of some goods and services. Government intervention is therefore desirable to clarify and enforce property rights, and to provide public goods that would not be provided in efficient amounts by the private sector. Another role of government is to correct for positive and negative externalities in order to improve productive efficiency. Other possible roles for government in market economies include maintaining competition, redistributing income and stabilizing the economy.

Reasoning

People respond predictably to positive and negative incentives. In the cases of public goods and positive externalities, people have incentives to be *free riders*. A free rider is a person who receives the benefit of a good but does not pay for it because the free rider cannot be excluded from consuming the good. This leads to the underproduction of public goods when the decision about how much to produce is left to free markets. In the case of negative externalities, people have incentives to impose some of their costs on others, leading to overproduction when the quantity of goods to produce is left to free markets. These are some of the situations that may call for government intervention if the benefits of the intervention outweigh the costs.

CONCEPTS

Externality
Market failure
Private-property rights
Public good
Role of government in a market economy

CONTENT STANDARDS

4. People respond predictably to positive and negative incentives.

16. There is an economic role for government to play in a market economy whenever the benefits of a government policy outweigh its costs. Governments often provide for national defense, address environmental concerns, define and protect property rights, and attempt to make markets more competitive. Most government policies also redistribute income.

OBJECTIVES

Students will
1. Analyze the economic functions of government in a market economy.

2. Participate in an activity demonstrating the characteristics of and problems with public goods.

3. Participate in or observe an activity to determine when negative externalities are present and propose solutions for negative externalities.

LESSON DESCRIPTION

Students brainstorm suggestions about which functions government should perform in a market economy and compare their suggestions with categories economists frequently use. They participate in a quiz activity that shows the characteristics of public goods and explains why certain public goods are best provided by the government. They next participate in or observe a short play to determine when negative externalities exist and suggest solutions for the problem.

Note: The two activities in this lesson may be conducted separately in different lessons.

TIME REQUIRED

75 minutes

MATERIALS

1. Visuals 5.1, 5.2, 5.3 and 5.4

2. A printed copy of Visual 5.2, folded and stapled

3. A copy of Activity 5.1 for each student.

4. **(Optional)** Props to use as costumes, garbage and so on for the "Life on Dismal Lake" activity

PROCEDURE

1. Ask the students to brainstorm ideas about what they think the government should do or what functions they think the government should perform. Accept all serious answers, and write them on the board or overhead projector. *Answers will vary. They will likely mention things such as building roads, providing education, helping poor people, defending the country, providing police protection, etc.*

2. Remind the students that one of the characteristics of a market economy is a limited role for government. That is, in market economies most decisions are made by individual consumers and by producers or privately owned businesses. A pure market economy is sometimes referred to as a *laissez-faire system*, meaning that the government doesn't interfere in economic activities and lets the economy run itself. But even so, economists generally agree that there are important roles for the government to play in market economies. Economists don't always agree, however, about what all of these roles are or the extent of these roles. (Lesson 4 discusses

the characteristics of a market economy in some detail.)

3. Display Visual 5.1, and tell the students that many economists believe these are the economic functions government should perform in a market economy. Announce that the students will later take part in two activities that demonstrate the economic functions of government. Briefly discuss the functions, and relate them to the list the students generated.

    A. Provide a Legal System. The government needs to provide a system of laws and courts to protect property rights. The right to own property is one of the most basic characteristics of market economies. (The importance of property rights is discussed in more detail in Lesson 4.)

    B. Provide Public Goods. Some goods, such as national defense, would not be provided in large-enough quantities by the private (non-government) sector of the economy. These goods are subject to free-rider problems: Once someone has provided the goods, others can use them without paying for them. These goods are called *public goods* and generally need to be provided by the government if people want enough of them.

    C. Correct Market Failures. Sometimes the prices and quantities of goods and services determined solely by markets are not the best for society. Environmental pollution is an example of an *external cost* or *negative externality*. If a steel factory disposes of its waste in the air and causes pollution, it imposes costs on others and therefore doesn't pay for all of its production costs itself. An example of an *external benefit* or *positive externality* is when a farmer sprays his or her trees to get rid of pests that damage not only his or her crops but also all of the crops in the area. Everyone in the area benefits from this spraying, even though others don't pay for it. These situations are examples of *market failures* because the farm and the factory do not produce an efficient amount of the goods and services involved.

When the decision about how much to produce is left entirely up to the markets, there's too much steel and too little pest spraying. Most economists agree that there is a role for the government to play in cases such as these.

D. Maintain Competition. Competition is important in market economies because it leads to lower production costs and prices. If businesses become monopolies, the benefits of competition are lost. There is a role for government to regulate some monopolies such as public utilities. Some economists also believe that the government should prevent monopolies from occurring or break them up when they do occur.

E. Redistribute Income. People, acting through their government, often decide it would be fair for the government to take income from some people and give it to others. Two examples of this are taxes and social-welfare programs. Although many people agree that this is a good idea, there are many different opinions about how to do this fairly.

F. Stabilize the Economy. Many economists believe the government should take an active role to try to achieve steady economic growth and low levels of unemployment and inflation. The government attempts to do this through *fiscal policy*: taxation and spending. In the United States, the Federal Reserve System, the country's central bank, conducts *monetary policy*, which seeks to stabilize the economy through control of the money supply.

PUBLIC-GOODS ACTIVITY

4. Inform the class that you are sorry you forgot to tell them before, but there will be a surprise quiz today. Hold up a folded and stapled copy of Visual 5.2, and tell them it includes both the quiz questions and the answers. Tell the students you are willing to sell copies of the questions and answers to anyone willing to pay $1. You will take an IOU. Anyone who buys the quiz and answers may use it to take the quiz. You will not let anyone who buys the quiz and answers share them with other students. Ask if there are any questions.

5. Ask for a show of hands: How many people are willing to pay $1 for the quiz? Write the number on the board. Now tell the class that you have decided it would be easier for you and require less paper – which is in short supply at school – if you put a transparency of Visual 5.2 (with the quiz questions and answers) on the overhead projector rather than giving copies to the students willing to pay $1. Display only the title of Visual 5.2 (with the questions and answers covered up) for all the students to see. Ask the students if they agree this is a good idea. *Responses will vary. Someone will eventually say that the students who didn't pay the $1 can still get the questions and answers, and it isn't fair to the students who will pay. Someone else may comment that they don't want to pay $1 any more if they can get the questions and answers without paying.*

6. Inform the students you are still willing to sell the quiz questions and answers for $1 before you pass out copies of the quiz to the class. If at least one student pays you, you will display the quiz and answers on the overhead projector. Ask how many students are willing to pay you $1 under these circumstances. Allow the students to ask questions and talk among themselves before asking for a show of hands. In response to questions, make it clear that all the students will be able to see the questions and answers whether they pay or not. Write the number of students now willing to pay $1 on the board. *Probably a few students will offer to pay $1 to make sure someone does, but the number should be a lot lower than before.*

7. Tell the class you've decided you don't need to give them the quiz, and they will all earn a perfect score. Display Visual 5.2, and briefly discuss the quiz and answers.

8. Discuss public goods with the class.

   A. Ask why more students were willing to buy the "Economic Quiz with Answers" the first time than the second time. *The first time, the information was available only to the students who paid for it. The second time those who didn't pay could still get the information.*

   B. Display and discuss Visual 5.3, "Public Goods," and relate the concepts to the quiz activity. *In the first round, the quiz questions and answers were private goods. Nonpayers could be excluded, and shared consumption was not allowed. A lot of people were willing to pay because this was the only way they could get the good. In the second round, the quiz questions and answers became a public good, so many students were no longer willing to pay. Everyone could consume the good at the same time, and no one could be excluded from consuming it. Students had incentives to be nonpayers or free riders.*

   C. Point out that the quiz activity demonstrates why it is necessary to have the government provide public goods such as national defense. Many people are not willing to pay for public goods on their own. They know they can consume the goods without paying for them, so private businesses have no incentives to provide them. Therefore, the government provides certain goods through tax revenue.

   D. You may want to discuss public goods in more detail. Explain that economists use the term *public goods* only for goods with the characteristics of shared consumption and nonexclusion. However, the government also provides many goods and services that do not have these characteristics – for example, public housing for the poor or dormitories at public universities. There are few examples of *pure* public goods, but many goods have some public-goods characteristics and are therefore provided by government. Examples are police and fire protection, wilderness areas, weather forecasts, lighthouses and streetlights. Public goods are a type of positive externality, which is discussed on Visuals 5.1 and 5.4.

EXTERNALITY ACTIVITY

9. Display Visual 5.4, "Externalities." Read and discuss the ideas with the students. You may want to point out that public goods are a type of positive externality. Announce that they will now take part in an activity that helps them recognize externality problems. The name of the activity is "Life on Dismal Lake." (If you don't want to do this activity as a role-play, you could distribute copies of Activity 5.1 to each student to read and then discuss the questions. If you do this as a role-play, don't distribute Activity 5.1 until Procedure 13.)

10. Select four students to play parts in Act I in "Life on Dismal Lake." One student will play the part of Mama Smith, another Papa Smith and two will play the parts of the Smiths' teenage children. You may give the students props to use for costumes and garbage and spread aluminum foil on the floor to represent the lake. Tell the actors to interpret their roles as you or a student read Act I from Activity 5.1. Read slowly to the class, pausing after each sentence so the Smith family can act out the events.

11. Select one more student to play the role of Snively Whiplash, and continue with Act II of the scenario. Remember to read slowly and pause after each sentence.

12. Select 15 more students to participate in the play as the 15 new families who move to the lake. Then read Act III slowly, pausing after each sentence.

13. Distribute copies of Activity 5.1 to the students so that they will have the text of the scenario to work with, and discuss "Life on Dismal Lake" by answering the questions that follow each act.

Act I: Only the Smith family lives on the lake. Is there an externality problem (are any costs imposed on others outside the family) when the children throw the trash in the lake? How should this problem be solved? *No external costs were imposed on others outside the Smith family. The Smiths bear all of the costs of the pollution themselves because no one else has property rights to the lake. The problem is solved when they eventually decide to take care of the pollution themselves and stop polluting the lake and clean it up. This is usually, but not always, what happens when people think about taking care of their own property and homes. Some students may argue that the Smith teenagers imposed external costs on their parents. If we treat the family as a single economic unit, as economists usually do, then there is no externality problem because there is no third party being hurt by the pollution.*

Act II: Now both the Smiths and Whiplash live on the lake. Is there an externality problem when Whiplash throws garbage into the lake? How should this problem be solved? *When Whiplash pollutes the lake, external costs are imposed on the Smiths, who also live on the lake. To solve the problem, some students will probably suggest that the Smiths go to the police or courts to make Whiplash stop polluting. Point out that they are defining a role for government to solve the problem. Government intervention can be costly, because it takes tax dollars. The Smiths may need to hire a lawyer if they take Mr. Whiplash to court.*

Ask if there is any way to solve the problem without involving government. *Some students will suggest that since the Smiths know who is doing the polluting, they could talk to Whiplash and try to convince him to stop.*

Ask whether Whiplash has any incentives to stop polluting if he is not forced to do so. *Some students may say yes because he would be embarrassed at being caught and not being a good citizen. Others may argue that he would have no incentives to stop unless the government forced him to do so.*

Ask what would happen if the courts decided that Whiplash had a right to pollute the lake because he owned most of it. What could the Smiths do then? *They could move, clean the lake themselves, take Whiplash's garbage out to the road for pick up themselves or even pay Whiplash to stop polluting. Students may say it isn't fair to have the Smiths rather than Whiplash pay. Remind them that the Smiths are the ones who want the lake clean and if they didn't live on the lake, there would not be an externality problem.*

Act III: Now 16 families live on the lake. Is there an externality problem when some unidentified families throw garbage into the lake? How can this problem be solved? *When 16 families live on the lake, there is an externality problem caused by those who are polluting. Students will probably suggest that the government pass laws or use other types of intervention to solve the problem. With more people, it is much more difficult to determine who is doing the polluting and how much, and it would be difficult to work out agreements among the families to pay for the pollution damages. In other words, the more people involved, the more likely direct government rules and enforcement are called for.*

14. To conclude the lesson, point out that most externality problems occur when property rights are poorly defined and enforced. Such problems can also arise when it is difficult to define and enforce these rights. For example, most pollution problems

involve air, oceans, rivers and streams, which nobody really owns. Similarly, public parks are more often littered than people's front yards, especially in neighborhoods with single-family, owner-occupied homes.

CLOSURE

Review Visual 5.1, "The Role of Government in a Market Economy," with the students. Ask them to give examples of each of the functions of government on the list.

VISUAL 5.1
THE ROLE OF GOVERNMENT IN A MARKET ECONOMY

A. **Provide a Legal System** to make and enforce laws and to protect private property rights.

B. **Provide Public Goods** that individuals or private businesses wouldn't provide.

C. **Correct Market Failures** such as external costs and external benefits.

D. **Maintain Competition** by regulating monopolies.

E. **Redistribute Income** by taxing those with larger incomes and helping those in need.

F. **Stabilize the Economy** by reducing unemployment and inflation, and promoting economic growth.

VISUAL 5.2
ECONOMIC QUIZ WITH ANSWERS

1. Who wrote, "In this world nothing is certain but death and taxes"?

   Benjamin Franklin

2. Who was the author of *The Wealth of Nations*?

   Adam Smith

3. Who wrote *The General Theory of Employment, Interest and Money*?

   John Maynard Keynes

4. What does TNSTAAFL stand for?

   There's no such thing as a free lunch.

VISUAL 5.3
PUBLIC GOODS

Most goods and services produced in market economies are *private goods and services*. The consumers who purchase these goods consume these goods; for example, a hamburger is a private good. National defense is an example of a public good. *Public goods* differ from private goods because they have these characteristics:

Shared consumption
When one person consumes a public good, it does not prevent others from also consuming the good.

Nonexclusion
Once a public good is produced, it is difficult or impossible to exclude others from consuming the good, even if they didn't pay for it.

Because people can consume public goods without paying for them (called the *free-rider problem*), private businesses do not have incentives to produce enough public goods. Therefore, the government often provides them, through tax dollars, if people want them.

VISUAL 5.4
EXTERNALITIES

Market prices usually reflect the costs producers pay to produce goods and the benefits consumers receive from the good. A kind of *market failure* occurs when market prices fail to reflect all the costs and all the benefits involved. This kind of market failure is called an *externality problem.*

Externalities exist when some of the costs or benefits associated with the production or consumption of a product spill over to third parties, who do not produce or pay to consume the product.

Positive externalities are *benefits* enjoyed by someone who does not produce or pay to consume a product. An example of a positive externality is elementary education, because society as a whole benefits when others can read and write. The government provides free public education to encourage everyone to be educated. Positive externalities often call for government subsidies or government provision.

Negative externalities are *costs* paid by someone who does not produce or pay to consume a product. An example of a negative externality is air pollution caused by cigarette smoking: Because others suffer from the smoke, the government may pass laws preventing smoking in certain places. Negative externalities often call for the government to clearly define property rights, or for corrective government measures such as taxation or fines.

ACTIVITY 5.1
LIFE ON DISMAL LAKE

Act I

The Smith family owns all the land around 100-acre Dismal Lake and builds its home on the eastern edge of the lake. Life is very pleasant for the first year. Then, unknown to Mama and Papa, the Smith children begin throwing the family garbage in the lake when they take it out once a week, because this is easier than carrying the bags all the way to the road for the county trash trucks to pick up. After a few months the lake begins to stink, and Mama and Papa Smith discover where the garbage has been going. The Smith children are now dismal because they must clean up the lake instead of going out with their friends for the next four weekends.

Question for discussion
Only the Smith family lives on the lake. Is there an externality problem (i.e., are any costs imposed on others outside the family) when the children throw the trash in the lake? How should this problem be solved?

Act II

When the Smith children go to college, Mama and Papa Smith sell all the land around Dismal Lake except their one-acre homestead to a man named Snively Whiplash. Whiplash builds a home on the western edge of the lake and immediately starts throwing garbage into the lake instead of taking it out to the road for the county trash service.

Question for discussion
Now both the Smiths and Whiplash live on the lake. Is there an externality problem when Whiplash throws garbage into the lake? How should this problem be solved?

Act III

One year later Whiplash, who turns out to be an unscrupulous land developer, stops throwing trash in Dismal Lake and cleans it up. Then he subdivides the land, sells homestead plots to 15 families for $100,000 each and moves away. The 15 new owners build large houses on their lots. After a few months, garbage shows up on and around Dismal Lake again – this time from two or more unidentified families. The Smiths call a neighborhood meeting to discuss the problem. At the meeting, four families accuse five other families of throwing garbage in the lake. The accused families deny the charges and accuse other families. The meeting breaks up with everyone shouting at each other. Dismal Lake continues to be a smelly, dismal place.

Question for discussion
Now 16 families live on the lake. Is there an externality problem when some unidentified families throw garbage into the lake? How can this problem be solved?

Lesson 6 - The Economic Way of Thinking: Three Activities to Demonstrate Marginal Analysis

INTRODUCTION

Economics

In economics, *marginal* refers to one more unit of something. Marginal analysis has many applications and is useful in both personal and social decision making. Should a firm produce a few more or a few less units of output in order to maximize its profits? Should a consumer buy a bit more of this and bit less of that to be as satisfied as possible with the expenditure? Is the marginal or additional value to a firm of hiring more workers greater than the marginal or additional cost of hiring those workers? These are examples of decisions applying marginal analysis.

Another common use of the term marginal in economics has to do with *diminishing marginal returns*. When capital resources are fixed, the law of diminishing marginal returns predicts that the productivity of labor will eventually fall as additional (marginal) workers are used in the production process. Similarly, the law of *diminishing marginal utility* predicts that marginal value or satisfaction will decrease as additional units of a good or service are consumed.

Reasoning

Comparing marginal benefits with marginal costs is an important part of the economic way of thinking and leads to rational decision making for consumers, firms and governments. Choices are rarely all-or-nothing propositions but usually concern marginal or incremental changes. Rational economic decision making says that if the marginal benefits of an action are greater than the marginal costs, the action should be undertaken. If the marginal costs are greater than the marginal benefits, the action should not be undertaken. Economists often state these rules by saying that actions should be undertaken until the marginal benefits are equal to the marginal costs.

CONCEPTS

Diminishing marginal returns
Diminishing marginal utility
Marginal analysis
Marginal benefits and marginal costs
Opportunity cost
Scarcity
Specialization and division of labor

CONTENT STANDARDS

2. Effective decision making requires comparing the additional costs of alternatives with the additional benefits. Most choices involve doing a little more or a little less of something; few choices are all-or-nothing decisions.

6. When individuals, regions and nations specialize in what they can produce at the lowest cost and then trade with others, both production and consumption increase.

17. Costs of government policies sometimes exceed benefits. This may occur because of incentives facing voters, government officials and government employees, because of actions by special interest groups that can impose costs on the general public, or because social goals other than economic efficiency are being pursued.

OBJECTIVES

Students will

1. Participate in or observe a production activity to understand the law of diminishing marginal returns.

2. Participate in or observe a consumption activity to understand the law of diminishing marginal utility.

3. Participate in or observe an activity relating to environmental cleanup to understand the importance of comparing marginal benefits with marginal costs.

LESSON DESCRIPTION

This lesson consists of three activities that demonstrate different applications of marginal analysis. You may use the activities separately or do them together in one class period. In the first activity, the students produce a good and demonstrate the law of diminishing marginal returns. In the second activity, a student consumes a good and demonstrates the law of diminishing marginal utility. In the third activity, the students participate in an environmental-cleanup project that demonstrates the importance of comparing marginal benefits with marginal costs when making decisions.

TIME REQUIRED

Each of the three activities takes about 20 minutes.

MATERIALS

Fluffernutter Production Activity
1. Visuals 6.1 and 6.2

2. A large jar of peanut butter, a large jar of marshmallow cream, a large box of graham crackers, two sturdy knives, a package of paper plates and a roll of paper towels

Diminishing Marginal Utility Activity
1. Visual 6.3

2. A supply of water and a small paper cup (to hold about two or three ounces)

"How Clean Is Clean Enough?" Activity
1. Visuals 6.4 and 6.5

2. A very dirty small rug or carpet sample: Stain with grape juice or coffee. Grind in things such as dust, coffee grounds and sand. Cover with crushed leaves and confetti from a hole-punch. Sprinkle with items such as soda bottles and cans. Some items should be easy to clean and others difficult or impossible to clean.

3. A pile of play money or beans or some other item to represent money

4. Several plastic grocery bags

5. Plastic gloves

PROCEDURE
FLUFFERNUTTER PRODUCTION ACTIVITY

1. Announce that the class will observe an important economic law by watching or participating in a simple production activity. At a small desk or table at the front of the room, demonstrate how to produce a fluffernutter using the following steps:
   A. Break a large graham cracker into smaller rectangles.
   B. Spread one rectangle with peanut butter using one knife. Emphasize that the students must use knives to spread the peanut butter and marshmallow cream, i.e., they cannot use crackers to spread the materials on other crackers.
   C. Spread another rectangle with marshmallow cream using another knife.
   D. Stack the two rectangles together to make a fluffernutter and place it on a paper plate.
   Students may produce other products such as paper pizzas or greeting cards instead of fluffernutters. The important thing is to have one or more fixed factors of production, such as knives and table size in the fluffernutter example.

2. Select a student volunteer to come to the front of the room and be a fluffernutter-maker. Appoint a quality-control inspector and a timekeeper with a loud voice and a watch. Tell the student to make as many fluffernutters as possible in exactly one minute. When the minute is up, ask the quality-control inspector to quickly inspect the products and to separate finished, acceptable fluffernutters from those that are unacceptable or unfinished. (You may want to discuss acceptable quality-control standards, as sometimes inspectors have a tendency to be too picky.) Remove both finished and unfinished fluffernutters from the table.

3. Display Visual 6.1 and fill in the second row, which corresponds to one worker. Record in the second column the number of acceptable fluffernutters the student produced. Read the definition of marginal output, and fill in the marginal output in the third column. For example, if the student produced two acceptable fluffernutters, total output would be two and marginal output would also be two, since total output changed from zero to two.

4. Ask the fluffernutter-maker to select another student to join in the production process. Tell them to make as many fluffernutters as they can in one minute. When the minute is up, ask the quality-control inspector to determine how many acceptable fluffernutters the students produced. Fill in the next row on Visual 6.1. Set aside both finished and unfinished fluffernutters in another part of the room.

5. Repeat step four several more times, adding one worker at a time. Conduct enough rounds until diminishing marginal returns have clearly set in. (This occurs when the numbers in the third column begin to decrease.) During the additional rounds, do not give workers additional knives or allow them to change the size of the workspace. However, they should be allowed to wipe off their hands between rounds with the paper towels if they so request. (Making fluffernutters can be messy.) Be sure to remove finished and partially finished products between rounds.

6. **Increasing Marginal Returns:** When you have finished the desired number of rounds, pass around the fluffernutters for the students to sample. Ask how specialization and division of labor affected total output. *Probably as more students were added to the production process, at first they specialized and divided tasks to become more efficient. This most likely caused total output to increase and increasing returns to set*

in. Increasing returns occur when the numbers in the third column increase, indicating that a marginal or additional worker adds more to total output than the prior worker.

7. **Diminishing Marginal Returns:** Ask the students to look at column three on Visual 6.1, showing marginal output. Ask why marginal output eventually decreased. *Answers will vary. Someone will eventually suggest that there weren't enough knives for additional students, and they were becoming crowded, so adding more workers didn't lead to as much additional (marginal) output.*
Note: If the numbers your class generated do not clearly show diminishing marginal returns, you may want to evaluate the following production numbers for zero to six workers from another class. Total product: 0, 2, 5, 9, 12, 13, 13. Marginal product: first worker 2, then 3, 4, 3, 1, 0. In this case, increasing returns occur with the second and third workers, and diminishing returns set in with the fourth worker.

8. Tell the students they have observed the law of diminishing marginal returns, which occurs with production processes when at least one resource is fixed. Display Visual 6.2 and discuss how the law was demonstrated with fluffernutter production. The variable resource was the number of workers. Fixed resources were the number of knives and the size of the workspace (the table or desk). As more and more workers were added, the additional fluffernutters produced per additional worker eventually declined, as shown in column three. In the example given in step seven where marginal output is 2, 3, 4, 3, 1, 0, diminishing marginal returns set in with the fourth worker (because three is less than four). This occurred because of the fixed resource – the knives – and not because the fourth worker was lazy or incompetent compared with the others.

9. **(Optional)** You may want to discuss how diminishing marginal returns relate to the number of workers a firm will hire. This depends on the selling price of the product and the wages and other costs of hiring workers, as well as the marginal product of labor. As long as hiring a marginal or additional worker brings in more benefits than costs to the firm, he or she will be hired, even though diminishing marginal returns have set in.

DIMINISHING MARGINAL UTILITY ACTIVITY

1. Display a large bottle or pitcher of water and ask if anyone is thirsty. Select a student volunteer to come to the front of the room to both quench his or her thirst and demonstrate an important economic law.

    A. Fill a small cup with water. The student may refill the cup and drink as much water as he or she wants.

    B. On the board or overhead projector, quickly write one column of numbers from 1-15 for each cup of water the student chooses to consume. Then label another column for the student's satisfaction with each additional (marginal) cup of water consumed.

    C. Each time the student finishes drinking a cup of water, have him or her state the overall satisfaction or utility received from drinking that water on a scale of one to 10. You or the student should record the number on the board or overhead projector. For example, if the student is very thirsty and the first cup of water is very satisfying, record a 10. If the second cup is very satisfying but not as satisfying as the first, record an eight and so on.

    D. Continue to record the number that shows the satisfaction the student receives from consuming each subsequent cup of water. Encourage the student to drink enough water so his or her satisfaction level decreases, but allow him or her to stop whenever he or she wants.

2. When the student has finished, discuss what happened. Point out that the numbers recorded in the second column represent the marginal value (additional satisfaction or utility) from each marginal (additional) cup of water. No doubt the student's level of satisfaction will have decreased as he or she consumed more and more water. For example, the satisfaction levels may have been 10, 9, 6, 4, 2, 1. This demonstrates the law of diminishing marginal utility.

3. Display and discuss Visual 6.3, "The Law of Diminishing Marginal Value" (often called diminishing marginal utility). Discuss the definition with the students and explain how it relates to the activity. Ask the students to evaluate this statement: "You **can** have too much of a good thing." *Answers will vary. The idea is that because of diminishing marginal utility, eventually people will choose to consume more of another good rather than increasing amounts of the first good, even if they really like the first good a lot.*

4. **(Optional)** You may want to point out that diminishing marginal value is one of the reasons underlying the downward-sloping demand curve. Point out that the levels of satisfaction the student recorded may indicate his or her willingness to pay for additional glasses of water. Consumers generally receive less satisfaction from additional units of a good consumed and therefore are willing to pay less for additional units. This is what a downward-sloping demand curve reflects, with price on the vertical axis and quantity on the horizontal axis.

"HOW CLEAN IS CLEAN ENOUGH?" ACTIVITY

1. Before class begins, prepare a dirty rug as described under Materials. Place the rug where the students can see it when they enter the classroom.

2. Display Visual 6.4, "Environmental Statements." Ask how many students agree with Statement 1 and how many agree with Statement 2. Ask a few students to explain their answers.

3. Remind the students that productive resources are scarce. Show the class the pile of play money (or beans) and say it represents the annual budget of a local government. Ask the students to suggest uses for the money, and write their suggestions on the board. *Answers will vary, but may include education, police and fire protection, salaries for those who work for the government and programs for the poor.*
If the students do not suggest "cleaning the environment" as an alternative, add this to the list.

4. Quickly divide the money into piles representing possible expenditures on the different categories suggested. Have about eight or 10 pieces of money in the pile for cleaning the environment.

5. Tell the students you will conduct a classroom experiment involving the use of scarce resources and cleaning the environment. Ask for two student volunteers to help clean the dirty rug, which represents a polluted lake. The students will have 20 seconds to make the rug as clean as they can. They must pick up the trash and deposit it into a bag. To make the experiment work, tell the students they cannot simply pick up the rug and pour off the trash into the bag. Also, they cannot use pieces of trash to sweep away, collect or pick up other pieces of trash. They are to use only their hands to pick up the trash. You may give them plastic gloves to wear if you want. Appoint a timekeeper with a watch that shows seconds. Have the rest of the class sit or stand so they can observe the cleanup. At the end of 20 seconds, look at the bag of trash the students collected and the trash that remains on the rug. Ask the class if they think the rug

is clean. Most will say no. Pay the student volunteers for their work with some of the play money from the pile designated for cleaning the environment.

6. Conduct four or five more 20-second rounds, each time giving the student volunteers a new bag, paying them the same amount of play money as in the first round, and asking the class if they think the rug is clean. It will be clear that the bags of trash the student volunteers collect are decreasing with each round, although the cost in terms of the money spent is the same. When the play money in the clean-the-environment pile is gone, ask the students if they believe it is worth it to continue cleaning the rug. Ask what it would take to completely clean the rug. *Answers will vary. Some students will probably say the rug is clean enough, while others will say the environment should be perfectly clean.*

7. Point out that continuing to clean the rug (lake) means resources will have to be allocated from other uses the class listed earlier. Ask the students to identify the opportunity cost of cleaning the environment in terms of what they must give up.

8. Display Visual 6.5. Tell the students that the economic way of thinking requires measuring the marginal (additional) benefits of an action with the marginal (additional) costs. *Students may ask what to do if the marginal benefits are just equal to the marginal costs. Technically, the decision maker would be indifferent at this point. But economists often state the rule as doing something until the marginal benefits equal the marginal costs, because you wouldn't stop before this point or go beyond this point.*

9. In this experiment, the marginal benefits – reducing pollution – were measured by the amount of trash collected during each 20-second round. The marginal costs were

measured by the payout to the students who cleaned the rug. The costs are opportunity costs, as money used to clean the environment could also be used for other things. Discuss issues such as these:

   A. Given that the marginal benefits (the amount of trash collected) decreased with each round, might there come a time when the marginal costs of cleaning the rug (or the environment) were greater than the marginal benefits?

   B. In the extreme, what if the last bit of pollution in the lake were doing very little harm and it would be very, very expensive to locate and remove it? Could the money be better spent to improve schools or provide more police protection?

10. Display Visual 6.4 again and ask how many agree with Statement 1 and Statement 2. *Probably more students will agree with Statement 2 than before.* Emphasize that the point of the activity is to compare marginal benefits and marginal costs when deciding whether or not to do something. The point is *not* that a clean environment is not desirable.

CLOSURE

Review the idea with the students that the economic way of thinking requires *thinking at the margin*. Marginal analysis refers to evaluating what happens with one more unit of something. Ask the students to apply the concept to this example: Should they decide to sleep one additional hour tonight? *Answers will vary. Responses should include comparing the benefits of the additional sleep to the costs. The costs are opportunity costs and reflect the next best use of the student's time. If the benefits of the additional sleep are greater than the costs, they should sleep. If the costs – for example studying for a test – are greater than the benefits, they should study instead.*

VISUAL 6.1
PRODUCTION TABLE FOR FLUFFERNUTTERS

Number of Workers	Total Output	Marginal Output of an Additional Worker*
0	0	--
1		
2		
3		
4		
5		
6		
7		
8		

*In economics, *marginal* refers to one more unit of something. The marginal output of an additional worker means the change in total output that occurs when one more worker is added to produce something. Economists often call this the *marginal product of labor.*

VISUAL 6.2
THE LAW OF DIMINISHING MARGINAL RETURNS

When more and more units of a variable resource such as labor are added to a fixed resource such as capital, eventually the additional (marginal) output associated with the variable resource declines.

The law of diminishing marginal returns is observed in production processes when at least one resource is fixed – that is, it can't change during the time period in question.

VISUAL 6.3
THE LAW OF DIMINISHING MARGINAL VALUE

In a given time period, consumers generally receive less satisfaction from additional (marginal) units of a good consumed.

In other words, the more you consume of something, the less you value one additional unit of it.

VISUAL 6.4
ENVIRONMENTAL STATEMENTS

Statement 1

Local Lake is a disaster. It was once a beautiful, clean lake where you could drink the water safely. Now it is dirty from overuse, soil runoff and overflow from septic tanks. The County Council should clean the lake completely: 100% clean. The technology and know-how are available. There is no excuse for not doing the job completely.

Statement 2

We can clean up most of the pollution in the lake for one-third of what it would cost to make it *completely* clean. It may be too costly to clean the lake completely. Resources are scarce. If the County Council overspends for the environment, it can accomplish less in other areas that are important, too.

VISUAL 6.5
MARGINAL BENEFIT/MARGINAL COST RULE

The Economic Way of Thinking

If the marginal (additional) **benefit**
of an action is **greater than**
the marginal (additional) **cost**,
DO IT!

If the marginal **cost**
of an action is **greater than**
the marginal **benefit**,
DON'T DO IT!

Lesson 7 - A Market in Wheat

INTRODUCTION

Economics

The most important economic institution in a market economy is, not surprisingly, the *market*. In a market economy, *prices* allocate goods and services to the uses that individual buyers value most, according to what they are willing and able to pay for these goods and services. Prices are established through the interaction of buyers and sellers in the marketplace. Despite the importance of markets in a market economy, many people do not understand how they operate. Although most markets for goods and services are not as competitive as the wheat market in this activity, by playing "A Market in Wheat," the students gain a better understanding of how prices are determined in any market.

Reasoning

A fundamental assumption of economics is that people behave rationally. Therefore, buyers and sellers enter into exchange situations they believe will be beneficial to them. By participating in this simulation, the students will experience how markets work and how the forces of supply and demand establish prices.

CONCEPTS

Demand
Market
Market-clearing price, equilibrium price
Shortage
Supply
Surplus

CONTENT STANDARDS

7. Markets exist when buyers and sellers interact. This interaction determines market prices and thereby allocates scarce goods and services.

8. Prices send signals and provide incentives to buyers and sellers. When supply or demand changes, market prices adjust, affecting incentives.

OBJECTIVES

Students will
1. Participate in a simulation that demonstrates how the forces of supply and demand determine price and how changes in the price of a good or service affect the quantities demanded and supplied.

2. Define market-clearing price as the one price at which quantity demanded equals quantity supplied.

3. Graph data points for a demand curve and a supply curve and interpret the relationships demonstrated on the graph.

LESSON DESCRIPTION

Students participate as buyers or sellers in a simulation that shows how a competitive market works. They determine individual profits or losses from market transactions. They use data from the simulation to plot and interpret a graph showing supply and demand.
Note: This activity requires a class of at least 20 students to be effective. Up to 50 students can participate if your room is large enough.

TIME REQUIRED

75 minutes (60 minutes for three rounds of the simulation and discussion, and approximately 15 minutes for the follow-up activity described in "Closure")

MATERIALS

1. Visuals 7.1, 7.2 and 7.3
    (Optional) Make a Visual of Activity 7.4

2. One copy each of Activities 7.1 and 7.2, which contain 26 buy cards and 26 sell cards in the amounts shown below. Use different colors for the buy and sell cards. You may want to laminate the cards or glue them onto heavy card stock so you can use them multiple times.

SELL CARDS		BUY CARDS	
Price	Number	Price	Number
$1	0	$1	4
$2	2	$2	4
$3	2	$3	4
$4	2	$4	2
$5	2	$5	2
$6	2	$6	2
$7	4	$7	2
$8	4	$8	2
$9	4	$9	2
$10	4	$10	2

3. A copy of Activities 7.3, 7.4 and 7.5 for each student in the class

PROCEDURE

1. Distribute Activity 7.3, "How to Play a Market in Wheat," and read it aloud with the students.

2. Clear a large area in the classroom and designate it as the marketplace.

3. Have buy and sell cards ready; they should be kept in separate piles and shuffled between each round of play.
    Note: It is wise to appoint one or two students to handle the distribution and collection of the buy and sell cards during the game and another student to record each transaction on the classroom tally sheet, which is Visual 7.1.

4. Divide the class in half and have each group line up on opposite sides of the room. Tell the students that one group will be buyers and the other group will be sellers. Suggest that the students take note of those standing across the room from them, as these will be the students with whom they will be able to negotiate.

5. Distribute a score sheet to each student (Activity 7.4) and explain that they should use it to record every transaction they make. (If they need more space, tell them to use the back of the sheet or an additional piece of paper.) Review the details of the score sheet.

6. Make sure all the students understand that they will determine the profit or loss for each transaction by calculating the difference between the dollar amount on their card and the dollar amount of the deal they made.
    (Optional) Use a transparency of Activity 7.4 to discuss the score sheet.

7. Explain that you will conduct three rounds of trading, each lasting five minutes. After the first round, tell the students it was a practice round, but the next two rounds will count toward their final score for the day. As each round is conducted, announce how much time remains in one-minute intervals. Tell the students there will be a winner from each side: the buyer who makes the largest profit and the seller who makes the largest profit.
    (Optional) You may want to run only one or two rounds if time is short and the students understand the concept.

8. Use Visual 7.1 to record transactions. As described in Activity 7.3, buyers should report transactions to the recorder before getting a new card. Make sure the overhead remains on as tallies are made.

9. After each trading round, including the practice round, allow the students time to calculate their profits or losses. After all three rounds have been completed, have the students calculate their total profit or loss for Rounds 2 and 3 combined.

10. During the time between trading rounds, you may want to discuss the following strategies with the students.

 A. To make a large profit, should you be making many or few transactions? *Often the students who make the most transactions also make the largest profit.*

 B. Should you let other students see the information on your card? *No, you will lose the power to negotiate if the other party knows the point at which you will drop out of the negotiating process.*

 C. Do you have to make a profit on every transaction to have a profit at the end? *No. Again, more transactions generally garner more profit. Taking a loss on a particular transaction may be wise because the player will get a new card.*

 D. Should you watch the classroom tally sheet on the overhead during the trading rounds? *Yes, it allows you to know at what prices transactions are being made as well as the prices where negotiation would be fruitless.*

11. After the students have calculated their total profit and/or loss from Rounds 2 and 3, conduct the postgame discussion. Ask some or all of the following questions:

 A. At what price was wheat most frequently sold in each round? *Have the students examine their score sheets and the classroom tally sheet on the overhead. This price, which should be around $6, is known as the market-clearing or equilibrium price.*

 B. This price is known as the market-clearing or equilibrium price. Why would economists call it the market-clearing price? *Answers may vary but should include some mention that it repre-*

sents the price at which the number of buyers willing to buy was the same as the number of sellers willing to sell.

 C. In which round did the greatest spread in prices occur? *Examine the data, but this probably occurred in the earlier rounds.*

 D. Why did the prices become more clustered together in the later rounds? *Greater available information is the most likely cause. Markets tend to move toward an equilibrium price as buyers and sellers obtain information about the quantity of products available at different prices.*

 E. Did buyers or sellers determine the price for wheat? *Both buyers and sellers determined the market price through their interaction in the marketplace.*

 F. How did competition among the sellers and the buyers influence the price? *Because of competition within both groups, no single buyer or seller controlled the price.*

 G. Remind the students that in the game they just played, there were an equal number of buyers and sellers. What would happen if there were many more buyers than sellers? *If there were more buyers, the increased competition would drive the price of wheat higher. There would be even more people competing for a product that was now more scarce than before.* Depending on the time available and your students' level of understanding, you may want to conduct another round, with two-thirds of the class as buyers and one-third as sellers. Students should see a higher market price emerge on the classroom tally sheet.

 H. Why would the market-clearing price rise if there were more buyers than sellers? *If the price were to remain at the previous equilibrium, the wheat market would experience a shortage, where the quantity demanded was greater than the quantity supplied. To correct this shortage, the price would rise until the quantity demanded and supplied were again equal, thus creat-*

ing a new market-clearing price, or equilibrium.

I. What would be the effect of having more sellers than buyers? *The effect of additional sellers would be the exact opposite of the effect of having more buyers: A surplus would be created at the prior equilibrium price. The quantity supplied would be greater than the quantity demanded, forcing the market-clearing price to fall until a new equilibrium price was established.*

12. **(Optional)** Since actual consumers and producers are seldom required to buy or sell at a loss, this activity may be modified to allow students to turn in "losing" cards after attempting to obtain a trade for a specified time, e.g. two minutes. With this rule change, prices should converge sooner and show more cluster around the equilibrium price. If you use this version of the activity, cards turned in would not be recorded on the score sheet and references to losses in the materials would not be relevant.

CLOSURE

1. Distribute Activity 7.5, and display Visual 7.2 (they are the same). Tell the students that it is often helpful to use graphs to visualize supply and demand relationships. The demand and supply schedules on Activity 7.5 were determined from the set of 26 buy cards and 26 sell cards used in the game. Remind the students that the numbers in the demand and supply schedules are cumulative. For example, there are two buy cards for $10. These buyers would also be willing to buy at $9, so there are four buyers at $9, and so on.

2. Using Visual 7.2, help the students plot first the demand curve, and then the supply curve on the grid. Tell the students to make one point for each price-quantity combination and then connect the points for each curve.

3. Display Visual 7.3, showing the completed supply and demand curves for the market in wheat. Use the graph to discuss the concepts of equilibrium price, surpluses, shortages, the direct relationship between price and quantity supplied, and the inverse relationship between price and quantity demanded.

Students may ask why the quantity numbers on the graph are not the same as the number of trades they made at the various prices in the game they played. Remind them that the curves are drawn from the complete set of cards used once, whereas in their game they could turn in cards and go through the deck more than once. Also, the curves reflect what buyers and sellers were willing to trade for without losses, although in the game some students traded at a loss to get new cards.

4. Go over the answers to the questions on Activity 7.5.

   1. What is the equilibrium price? *$6.00*

   2. What prices would result in a surplus? *Any prices above $6.00*

   3. What prices would result in a shortage? *Any prices below $6.00*

VISUAL 7.1
CLASSROOM TALLY SHEET

Price	Round 1	Round 2	Round 3
$1			
$2			
$3			
$4			
$5			
$6			
$7			
$8			
$9			
$10			

VISUAL 7.2
WHEAT SUPPLY AND DEMAND

Given the buy cards and sell cards in the Market in Wheat game, the following demand schedule and supply schedule are generated. Use this information to plot a demand curve and a supply curve on the graph below and then answer the questions.

1. What is the equilibrium price?

2. What prices would result in a surplus?

3. What prices would result in a shortage?

Demand Schedule (Buy)		Supply Schedule (Sell)	
Price	Quantity Demanded	Price	Quantity Supplied
$1	26	$1	0
$2	22	$2	2
$3	18	$3	4
$4	14	$4	6
$5	12	$5	8
$6	10	$6	10
$7	8	$7	14
$8	6	$8	18
$9	4	$9	22
$10	2	$10	26

Wheat Supply and Demand

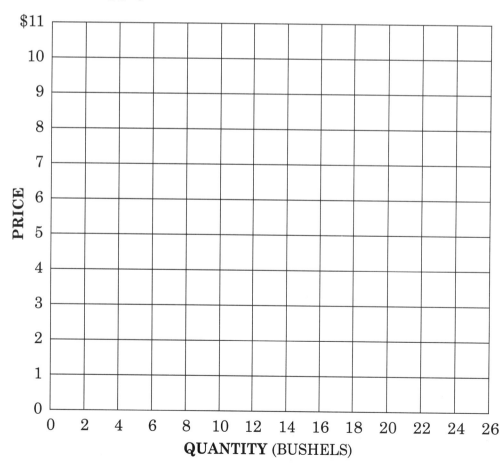

VISUAL 7.3
WHEAT SUPPLY AND DEMAND COMPLETED GRAPH

Wheat Supply and Demand

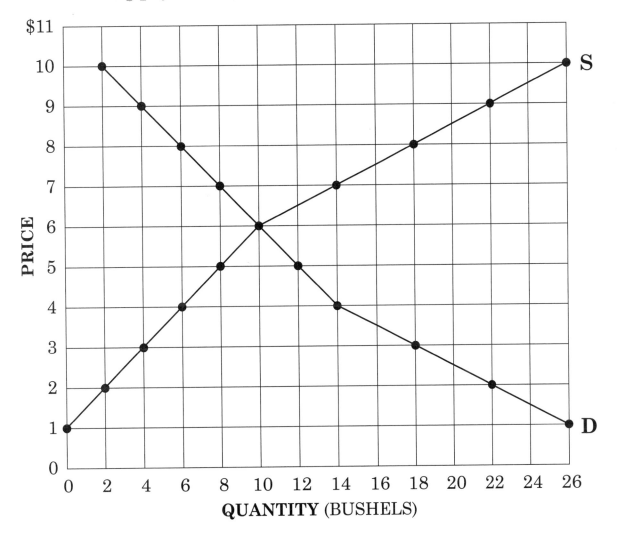

ACTIVITY 7.1
SELL CARDS FOR "A MARKET IN WHEAT"

You are authorized to **SELL** one bushel of wheat for as much as possible. If you sell for less than **$2.00** you will lose money.	You are authorized to **SELL** one bushel of wheat for as much as possible. If you sell for less than **$2.00** you will lose money.	You are authorized to **SELL** one bushel of wheat for as much as possible. If you sell for less than **$3.00** you will lose money.	You are authorized to **SELL** one bushel of wheat for as much as possible. If you sell for less than **$3.00** you will lose money.	You are authorized to **SELL** one bushel of wheat for as much as possible. If you sell for less than **$4.00** you will lose money.
You are authorized to **SELL** one bushel of wheat for as much as possible. If you sell for less than **$4.00** you will lose money.	You are authorized to **SELL** one bushel of wheat for as much as possible. If you sell for less than **$5.00** you will lose money.	You are authorized to **SELL** one bushel of wheat for as much as possible. If you sell for less than **$5.00** you will lose money.	You are authorized to **SELL** one bushel of wheat for as much as possible. If you sell for less than **$6.00** you will lose money.	You are authorized to **SELL** one bushel of wheat for as much as possible. If you sell for less than **$6.00** you will lose money.
You are authorized to **SELL** one bushel of wheat for as much as possible. If you sell for less than **$7.00** you will lose money.	You are authorized to **SELL** one bushel of wheat for as much as possible. If you sell for less than **$7.00** you will lose money.	You are authorized to **SELL** one bushel of wheat for as much as possible. If you sell for less than **$7.00** you will lose money.	You are authorized to **SELL** one bushel of wheat for as much as possible. If you sell for less than **$7.00** you will lose money.	

ACTIVITY 7.1, continued
SELL CARDS FOR "A MARKET IN WHEAT"

You are authorized to **SELL** one bushel of wheat for as much as possible. If you sell for less than **$8.00** you will lose money.	You are authorized to **SELL** one bushel of wheat for as much as possible. If you sell for less than **$8.00** you will lose money.	You are authorized to **SELL** one bushel of wheat for as much as possible. If you sell for less than **$8.00** you will lose money.	You are authorized to **SELL** one bushel of wheat for as much as possible. If you sell for less than **$8.00** you will lose money.
You are authorized to **SELL** one bushel of wheat for as much as possible. If you sell for less than **$9.00** you will lose money.	You are authorized to **SELL** one bushel of wheat for as much as possible. If you sell for less than **$9.00** you will lose money.	You are authorized to **SELL** one bushel of wheat for as much as possible. If you sell for less than **$9.00** you will lose money.	You are authorized to **SELL** one bushel of wheat for as much as possible. If you sell for less than **$9.00** you will lose money.
You are authorized to **SELL** one bushel of wheat for as much as possible. If you sell for less than **$10.00** you will lose money.	You are authorized to **SELL** one bushel of wheat for as much as possible. If you sell for less than **$10.00** you will lose money.	You are authorized to **SELL** one bushel of wheat for as much as possible. If you sell for less than **$10.00** you will lose money.	You are authorized to **SELL** one bushel of wheat for as much as possible. If you sell for less than **$10.00** you will lose money.

ACTIVITY 7.2
BUY CARDS FOR "A MARKET IN WHEAT"

You are authorized to **BUY** one bushel of wheat, paying as little as possible. If you spend more than **$1.00** you will lose money.	You are authorized to **BUY** one bushel of wheat, paying as little as possible. If you spend more than **$1.00** you will lose money.	You are authorized to **BUY** one bushel of wheat, paying as little as possible. If you spend more than **$1.00** you will lose money.	You are authorized to **BUY** one bushel of wheat, paying as little as possible. If you spend more than **$1.00** you will lose money.
You are authorized to **BUY** one bushel of wheat, paying as little as possible. If you spend more than **$2.00** you will lose money.	You are authorized to **BUY** one bushel of wheat, paying as little as possible. If you spend more than **$2.00** you will lose money.	You are authorized to **BUY** one bushel of wheat, paying as little as possible. If you spend more than **$2.00** you will lose money.	You are authorized to **BUY** one bushel of wheat, paying as little as possible. If you spend more than **$2.00** you will lose money.
You are authorized to **BUY** one bushel of wheat, paying as little as possible. If you spend more than **$3.00** you will lose money.	You are authorized to **BUY** one bushel of wheat, paying as little as possible. If you spend more than **$3.00** you will lose money.	You are authorized to **BUY** one bushel of wheat, paying as little as possible. If you spend more than **$3.00** you will lose money.	You are authorized to **BUY** one bushel of wheat, paying as little as possible. If you spend more than **$3.00** you will lose money.

ACTIVITY 7.2, continued
BUY CARDS FOR "A MARKET IN WHEAT"

You are authorized to **BUY** one bushel of wheat, paying as little as possible. If you spend more than **$4.00** you will lose money.	You are authorized to **BUY** one bushel of wheat, paying as little as possible. If you spend more than **$4.00** you will lose money.	You are authorized to **BUY** one bushel of wheat, paying as little as possible. If you spend more than **$5.00** you will lose money.	You are authorized to **BUY** one bushel of wheat, paying as little as possible. If you spend more than **$5.00** you will lose money.	You are authorized to **BUY** one bushel of wheat, paying as little as possible. If you spend more than **$6.00** you will lose money.
You are authorized to **BUY** one bushel of wheat, paying as little as possible. If you spend more than **$6.00** you will lose money.	You are authorized to **BUY** one bushel of wheat, paying as little as possible. If you spend more than **$7.00** you will lose money.	You are authorized to **BUY** one bushel of wheat, paying as little as possible. If you spend more than **$7.00** you will lose money.	You are authorized to **BUY** one bushel of wheat, paying as little as possible. If you spend more than **$8.00** you will lose money.	You are authorized to **BUY** one bushel of wheat, paying as little as possible. If you spend more than **$8.00** you will lose money.
You are authorized to **BUY** one bushel of wheat, paying as little as possible. If you spend more than **$9.00** you will lose money.	You are authorized to **BUY** one bushel of wheat, paying as little as possible. If you spend more than **$9.00** you will lose money.	You are authorized to **BUY** one bushel of wheat, paying as little as possible. If you spend more than **$10.00** you will lose money.	You are authorized to **BUY** one bushel of wheat, paying as little as possible. If you spend more than **$10.00** you will lose money.	

ACTIVITY 7.3
HOW TO PLAY "A MARKET IN WHEAT"

Read the following instructions carefully as your teacher reads them aloud. Note that buyers remain buyers throughout the game. Sellers remain sellers throughout the game.

1. Buyers will start the game with one buy-order card and one score sheet. The buy card will say, "You are authorized to BUY one bushel of wheat, paying as little as possible. If you spend more than _____, you will lose money." The exact price will be written on the buy card. Record the price of your buy order on your score sheet. When the round starts, try to buy at the lowest price you can. If you pay exactly the price written on your card, you will break even for that transaction. If you pay less than the price on your card, the difference is a profit. If you pay more than the price on your card, the difference is a loss. You may buy wheat at whatever dollar price you are able to negotiate in the marketplace. As soon as you have bought wheat, record the transaction on your score sheet. Then report the price you have negotiated to the recorder, who will keep a tally on the Classroom Tally Sheet. Turn in your buy card, receive a new card and begin the negotiation process anew. If you do not buy wheat during a round, you may return your buy card for a new card only after the round is finished.

2. Sellers will start with one sell-order card and one score sheet. The sell card will say, "You are authorized to SELL one bushel of wheat for as much as possible. If you sell for less than _____, you will lose money." The exact price will be written on the card. Record the price of your sell order on your score sheet. When the round starts, try to sell at the highest price you can. If you get exactly the price written on your card, you will break even for that transaction. If you get more than the price on your card, the difference is a profit. If you get less, the difference is a loss. You may sell wheat at whatever dollar price you are able to negotiate in the marketplace. As soon as you have sold wheat, record the transaction on your score sheet. Then turn in your sell card, receive a new card and begin the negotiation process anew. If you do not sell wheat during a round, you may return your sell card for a new card only after the round is finished.

3. When the teacher says, "The market is open," buyers and sellers should meet in the designated area and try to agree on a price for a bushel of wheat. Make all transactions in even dollar amounts for one bushel. Any buyer may talk with any seller.

4. The goal of buyers and sellers is to make as much money as they can. Buyers will do this by purchasing wheat for a lower price than the price shown on their card. Sellers make money by selling for a higher price than the price shown on their card.

5. Every time a price is agreed on and a sale is made, the buyer must report the price to the recorder, who will enter it on the Classroom Tally Sheet.

6. As soon as buyers and sellers receive new cards during a round, they should return to the marketplace and try to make another deal.

7. All students are free to make as many transactions in a round as time permits. Once the teacher says, "The market is closed," no further transactions will count.

ACTIVITY 7.4
SCORE SHEET FOR "A MARKET IN WHEAT"

Use this score sheet to keep track of your progress during the game. If you need more space for trades, use an additional piece of paper.

Circle one: I am a **BUYER**.   I am a **SELLER**.

Transaction	Price per Bushel On Card	In Transaction	Profit	Loss
1				
2				
3				
4				
5				
6					**Total** Round 1

Subtotals for Round 1   −   =

1				
2				
3				
4				
5				
6					**Total** Round 2

Subtotals for Round 2   −   =

1				
2				
3				
4				
5				
6					**Total** Round 3

Subtotals for Round 3   −   =

Total Rounds 2 & 3

ACTIVITY 7.5
WHEAT SUPPLY AND DEMAND

Given the buy cards and sell cards in the Market in Wheat game, the following demand schedule and supply schedule are generated. Use this information to plot a demand curve and a supply curve on the graph below and then answer the questions.

1. What is the equilibrium price?

2. What prices would result in a surplus?

3. What prices would result in a shortage?

Demand Schedule (Buy)		Supply Schedule (Sell)	
Price	Quantity Demanded	Price	Quantity Supplied
$1	26	$1	0
$2	22	$2	2
$3	18	$3	4
$4	14	$4	6
$5	12	$5	8
$6	10	$6	10
$7	8	$7	14
$8	6	$8	18
$9	4	$9	22
$10	2	$10	26

Wheat Supply and Demand

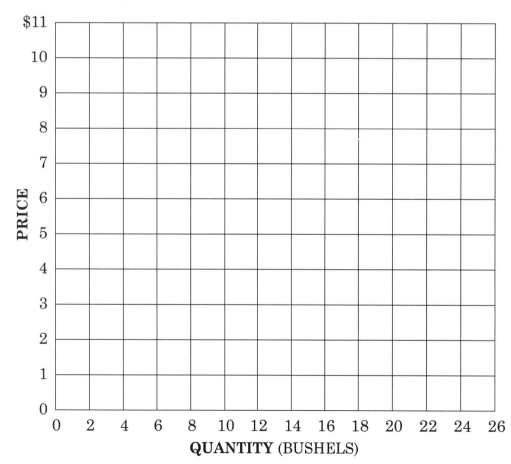

PRICE

QUANTITY (BUSHELS)

Lesson 8 - Productivity

INTRODUCTION

Economics

Although the problem of *scarcity* can never be eliminated, it can be moderated by finding ways to increase productivity. *Productivity* is the amount of goods and services produced (or *output*) per unit of productive resources used (or *input*) in a specific period of time such as one hour. Productivity can be increased by producing more goods and services with the same amount of resources, or by producing the same amount of goods and services with fewer resources. As productivity increases, production costs for each unit of a good or service decrease. This makes producers more competitive in the marketplace and translates into higher wages for workers at the national level. In individual markets, however, productivity increases can sometimes reduce the number of workers employed.

Reasoning

The choices producers make in attempting to boost productivity have far-reaching implications at the macro level. Over time, both personal and national living standards are directly related to labor productivity. For a country to be able to consume at high levels, it must have a highly productive labor force. Productivity can be increased by investing in capital goods such as factories, machines and tools. Individual workers can also increase productivity and enhance their own earning power by investing in their human capital through education and training.

CONCEPTS

Investment in capital goods
Investment in human capital
Productivity
Specialization and division of labor

CONTENT STANDARDS

6. When individuals, regions and nations specialize in what they can produce at the lowest cost and then trade with others, both production and consumption increase.

13. Income for most people is determined by the market value of the productive resources they sell. What workers earn depends, primarily, on the market value of what they produce and how productive they are.

15. Investment in factories, machinery, new technology, and the health, education and training of people can raise future standards of living.

OBJECTIVES

Students will
1. Define labor productivity as output per worker.

2. Explain how the division of labor and investment in capital goods improve productivity.

3. Explain why increased productivity is important to individuals and to the economy as a whole.

LESSON DESCRIPTION

Working in small groups, the students participate in a production simulation to determine the effects of specialization on labor productivity, the division of labor, and investment in human capital and capital goods.

TIME REQUIRED

60 minutes

MATERIALS

1. Visual 8.1

2. Large supply of 8.5" x 11" paper (scrap paper is fine)

3. Large supply of paper clips and pens

4. One copy of Activity 8.1 for each student

5. **(Optional)** One pair of gloves per group

PROCEDURE

1. Divide the class into book companies of four to five students per company. Have the students in each company arrange their desks to form a common work area. Ask the students to name their companies.

2. Tell the students they are going to produce books. Demonstrate how to construct a book as you explain the process. Tear a piece of paper in half, put the halves together, and tear the two halves in half again, making four quarters. Put the four quarters together and fold them in the middle, making a 14-page book plus front and back covers. Place a paper clip in the upper left-hand corner of the book to hold it together. Write the name of the company on the front cover and number the even (left-hand) interior pages from 2 through 14, placing each number in the bottom left-hand corner of the page. Explain that this is a completed book.
   (Optional) Have the students write "Quiz Book" on the cover, above the company name. Save completed books and use them later for pop quizzes.

3. Tell the students that they will have three minutes to produce as many books as they can. Inform them that you or students you choose will serve as the quality-control officers and inspect all finished books. Any books that do not meet production stan-

dards will be rejected and thrown away; only books that pass inspection and are accepted will count toward their total.

4. Distribute the paper, paper clips and one pen to each company. Allow time for each student in the class to make a practice book. Check to make sure all the students understand what they are to do. Discard all practice books at the end of this period.

ROUND 1

5. Inform the students that during Round 1, each worker in a company is a bookmaker. Each bookmaker produces the entire book alone. Bookmakers will share materials and capital goods (the pen), but not labor.

6. Give the companies three minutes to produce books. Quickly check each company's completed books and reject books that do not pass inspection. Discard all rejects and partially completed books.

7. Distribute a copy of Activity 8.1 to each student. Using Visual 8.1, go over the sample column with the class so all the groups understand how to record their data. Then ask the groups to calculate the Round 1 data for their company.
   A. Wages (line 2) are $1.00 per worker for each round.
   B. Rent (line 3) is $2.00 per round, no matter how many workers or desks the company has.
   C. Investment in capital (line 5) is the number of pens times 50 cents, which is the cost of one pen.
   D. The cost of materials (line 7) is 25 cents for the paper and paper clip used in each accepted book.
   E. Labor productivity (line 10) is the number of accepted books per worker in the three-minute time period.
   Note: The students may question why the costs of the materials for unfinished books are not included in line 7. Tell them that these costs are not included here to simplify the calculations in the activity and that

a real business would use the unfinished goods in inventory for future production. They may also question why only books that pass inspection (accepted books) are counted toward the productivity number. Tell them that a real business can sell only goods that meet required standards.

8. Ask the students, "What is another way you could organize this book production process?" *Students will usually suggest dividing the labor and specializing.*

ROUND 2

9. Once again, limit each company to only one pen, but allow the students to introduce specialization and division of labor. Allow time for the students to discuss breaking down the book production into a series of steps, and let each group member specialize in doing one or two specific steps. Point out that, as a specialist, each student will complete only a part of the production process.

10. Repeat step six and have the students record their data on Activity 8.1 in the Round 2 column. Use Visual 8.1 to help the students with the computations as necessary.

11. *If most companies do not experience an increase in productivity between Rounds 1 and 2, repeat Round 2.* This is often necessary because the specialists need practice in their specific assignments (investment in human capital), the assembly line needs to be reorganized or the specialists fail to cooperate.

ROUND 3

12. Now allow each company to "purchase" new capital resources: Offer to sell them as many pens as they want. Each pen costs 50 cents. Point out that pens are the companies' capital goods and that by purchasing them, a company would be investing in its physical capital. After the stu-

dents purchase pens, give the companies time to analyze their production process and reorganize if they so desire.

13. Repeat step six and have companies record their data on their Activity 8.1 handouts in the Round 3 column. Use Visual 8.1 to help with the computations as necessary.

14. Once the students have completed filling in their data, discuss the following:

    A. Explain that one definition of productivity is the ratio of the amount of output produced to the number of inputs used. Ask the students to explain their company's productivity ratio on line 10. *The productivity measure is labor productivity or output per worker in a three-minute time period. The number of accepted books produced in three minutes was divided by the number of workers in each company.* Point out that this ratio rises as productivity rises. Also, if we looked at labor productivity for all goods and services, not just books, as labor productivity increases, the goods and services available for people to consume would increase. This means that, on average, people's standard of living would increase.

    B. What happened to your productivity between Round 1 and Round 2? Between Round 2 and Round 3? Why did this occur? *In most cases, productivity should increase between Rounds 1 and 2 because of specialization and division of labor. Sometimes this does not happen, however, because of lack of skills, lack of cooperation among the assembly-line workers or inexperience. By Round 3, companies should have seen an increase in productivity as specialists have more practice and as the companies refine the assembly-line process.*

    C. What happened to the quality of the books between Rounds 1 and 3? *Typically, fewer and fewer books will be rejected, and the overall quality will improve.*

D. What effect did investing in additional capital goods (pens) in Round 3 have on productivity? *Investment in physical capital should have increased productivity.*

E. What effect did increased productivity have on average cost (line 9 of Activity 8.1)? *Average cost should decrease.* Why is this important? *Lower average cost means the producers can compete with other book companies more effectively, allowing them to stay in business longer and perhaps also earn higher profits.*

F. What effect will increased productivity have on wages in the long run? *More-productive workers will receive higher wages and have greater job security because they add more to the firm's revenue while lowering its average production costs. Less-productive workers may be fired and have to search for jobs. It is possible that if productivity increases for a particular product or factory, the number of workers employed will decrease if the firm cannot sell the additional output.*

G. What will happen if labor productivity increases in the overall economy? *At this level, productivity increases translate into higher average wages, more consumption and a higher material standard of living. Although there may be concerns about selling more units of some particular product made at one factory, there is not a concern about people wanting to buy more output of all goods and services.*

H. What costs did the companies incur by attempts to increase productivity? *Investing in additional capital resources – the extra pens – increased total costs but should lower average production costs if productivity increased.*

I. What are the advantages and disadvantages of specialization and division of labor? *Answers will vary but should include some mention of the following. Advantages: Specialists become very skilled at doing one step of the production process, product quality improves and productivity rises. Disadvantages: Workers may get easily bored with their jobs, problems occur when a specialist is absent and some workers may lose their old jobs because of productivity increases.*

J. What other things could the book companies have done to increase their productivity? *Provide practice time or on-the-job training for the specialists, which would be an investment in human capital, or invest in even more capital goods such as scissors or a paper cutter.*

K. What things should the company consider before investing in capital resources such as a paper cutter? *It should weigh the cost of the paper cutter, the cost of training workers to use the paper cutter and the risk involved in borrowing money to purchase it against the anticipated benefits of increased productivity.*

L. What is the opportunity cost of a firm's decision to invest in capital? *The opportunity cost is what the company would have done with the money had it not made a capital investment.*

M. Why would it be important for a nation to increase productivity? *Productivity increases can mean higher individual wage rates. If many of a country's people are receiving higher wages, this leads to increased consumption, increasing aggregate demand. This results in a rising gross domestic product because more people working with more money in their pockets purchase more and more goods and services. This raises the average standard of living in a country. Additionally, when productivity gains result in a greater quantity of goods and services being produced, a nation may be able to become more active in the international-trade* *arena, further raising the people's average standard of living.*

15. **(Optional rounds)** Implement the situations described below in one or more book companies, and then discuss changes in productivity.

   A. Allow companies to fire any workers they do not want to employ. Permit the fired workers to form new companies.

   B. Inform companies that a new government regulation requires all workers to wear gloves because of the toxic nature of the paper used in the production process. Distribute a pair of gloves to each of the companies.

   C. Inform the companies that a new union contract states each worker must receive a one-minute break during each production round.

CLOSURE

Discuss the following:

1. What is labor productivity?
   Output per worker

2. How do specialization, division of labor, and investment in human capital and capital goods affect productivity?
   Productivity increases.

3. What are the advantages to a firm of increasing productivity?
   Productivity increases lead to lower average production costs, and product quality typically improves.

4. Why is increasing productivity important to individuals and to the economy?
   Increasing productivity allows for higher consumption and higher income levels – in other words, a higher standard of living.

VISUAL 8.1
PRODUCTIVITY DATA

Name of book company _____

	Sample	Round 1	Round 2	Round 3
1. Number of workers	4			
2. Wages ($1 per worker)	$4.00			
3. Rent for factory (desks)	$2.00	$2.00	$2.00	$2.00
4. Capital goods (number of pens)	1			
5. Investment in capital goods ($0.50 per pen)	$0.50			
6. Number of accepted books	4			
7. Cost of materials ($0.25 per accepted book)	$1.00			
8. Total cost of accepted books *Wages (line 2) + rent (line 3) + investment in capital goods (line 5) + materials cost (line 7)*	$7.50			
9. Average cost per accepted book *Total cost (line 8) ÷ accepted books (line 6)*	$1.88			
10. Productivity: output per worker in 3 minutes *Accepted books (line 6) ÷ number of workers (line 1)*	1			

ACTIVITY 8.1
PRODUCTIVITY DATA

Name of book company _____

	Sample	Round 1	Round 2	Round 3
1. Number of workers	4			
2. Wages ($1 per worker)	$4.00			
3. Rent for factory (desks)	$2.00	$2.00	$2.00	$2.00
4. Capital goods (number of pens)	1			
5. Investment in capital goods ($0.50 per pen)	$0.50			
6. Number of accepted books	4			
7. Cost of materials ($0.25 per accepted book)	$1.00			
8. Total cost of accepted books *Wages (line 2) + rent (line 3) + investment in capital goods (line 5) + materials cost (line 7)*	$7.50			
9. Average cost per accepted book *Total cost (line 8) ÷ accepted books (line 6)*	$1.88			
10. Productivity: output per worker in 3 minutes *Accepted books (line 6) ÷ number of workers (line 1)*	1			

Lesson 9 - The Invention Convention

INTRODUCTION

Economics

In a market system, economic decisions are made in the marketplace through the interaction of producers and consumers. Businesses produce and sell the goods and services consumers desire. Businesses, or firms, must buy the *factors of production* (*resources* or *inputs*) such as labor and capital goods to produce the goods and services they sell to consumers. Firms do all this in an attempt to earn *profit*: the reward for entrepreneurs. Profit is determined by subtracting the *total cost* from the *total revenue* of the firm. When firms buy their inputs, they incur costs of production. Total cost is calculated by multiplying the prices of all the inputs used to produce each good or service by the number of that good or service produced. The firm's total revenue is calculated by multiplying the selling price of the product by the number of units sold. The primary objective of the firm is to maximize its profits – that is, to identify a selling price and production level where its total revenue exceeds its total cost by the greatest amount. If total cost is greater than total revenue, the firm suffers a loss.

Reasoning

Just like individuals, firms face choices all the time. First they must choose what to produce, trying to match their product to consumers' preferences. They must then decide how to produce their product. This includes deciding which resources to use in this process. These resources cost money, so firms must make their decisions carefully as they attempt to earn a profit. If their costs are too high and/or their revenue is too low, the firms will not be successful.

This lesson features material that was published previously in Coulson and McCorkle, *Economics in the Elementary Classroom*, SPEC Publishers Inc., Ballwin, Mo., 1992.

CONCEPTS

Costs of production
Loss
Profit
Total revenue

CONTENT STANDARDS

1. Productive resources are limited. Therefore, people cannot have all the goods and services they want; as a result, they must choose some things and give up others.

14. Entrepreneurs are people who take the risks of organizing productive resources to make goods and services. Profit is an important incentive that leads entrepreneurs to accept the risks of business failure.

OBJECTIVES

Students will

1. Explain that when producers purchase resources, they incur costs of production.

2. Define profit as total revenue minus total cost.

3. Compute profit and loss.

4. Define total revenue as a product's selling price multiplied by the quantity sold.

5. Define total cost as the per unit (average) resource cost multiplied by the quantity produced.

6. Explain that firms incur losses when their total cost exceeds total revenue.

LESSON DESCRIPTION

Working in small groups, the students simulate firms creating and producing new products. Using budget guidelines, they must decide which inputs they will purchase. They calculate their costs of production and then display their products to the class, discovering how many units they can "sell." They then calculate the profit or loss for their firm and compare results across the class.

TIME REQUIRED

60 minutes

MATERIALS

1. Visuals 9.1 and 9.2

2. A copy of Activities 9.1 and 9.2 for each student

3. Activity 9.3. Before the class begins, you will need to copy and cut out enough $5.00 bills for each student to get one bill.

4. Odds and ends such as cotton balls, egg cartons, paper, yarn, plastic cups, straws, markers, fabric remnants, fringe, pipe cleaners and berry baskets organized into resource bags. Prepare one resource bag for each group of students before class. Each bag should contain approximately the same resources.

5. A resource price list based on items compiled for the resource bags. This list will be posted on the board or written on a transparency.

6. (Optional) One envelope per group

7. (Optional) A small prize for members of the group earning the most profit

PROCEDURE

1. Arrange the students in small groups (three to four students is recommended, although you may want to have groups of differing numbers to vary the groups' labor costs). Ask the students about entrepreneurial experiences they have had such as running a lemonade stand, cutting the grass or baby sitting. Ask them what materials or supplies they needed before they could operate their business ventures and how much these materials cost. List the materials and costs on the board.

Explain that these are known as the costs of production for a business. Discuss how they determined what prices to charge in their ventures. Ask if they earned a profit.

2. Tell the students that in today's class, each group will simulate an actual business. They will invent a product that they believe other members of the class would desire to purchase. All members of the class will have an opportunity to decide which invention they would like to buy. Groups will also try to earn a profit in this activity, just as a real business firm would. You may want to offer an extra incentive in the form of a prize for the group that earns the most profit.

3. Distribute a resource bag to each group and a copy of Activity 9.1, "Calculating Costs of Production," to each student.

4. Explain that each resource bag contains items the group may use to assemble a prototype of its invention. Show them the resource price list on the board or on a transparency. **Note:** Make sure the

Sample Resource Price List	
Resource	**Price**
Glue stick	$ .50
Golf tee	.25
Felt-tip marker	.25
Paper plate	.75
Scissors	.75
Coffee can	1.00
Egg carton	1.00
Paper clip	.25
Aluminum foil	.25
Yarn	.25
Fabric remnant	.75
Plastic bag	.50
Rubber band	.25
Piece of ribbon	.50
Paper cup	.50
Paper lunch bag	.50
Labor (per worker)	.25
Rent for work space	.75

resource list totals well over $5.00 because this will be the selling price for each final product. The $5.00 price means that each group must use decision-making skills to decide which resources to use. The $5.00 price also will focus more group discussion on the total costs of production. See the "Sample Resource Price List" box on the previous page.

(Optional) You could use the resource list to discuss the difference between fixed and variable costs. Note that in this activity, the rent of $0.75 is treated as a per unit, or average, fixed cost.

5. Explain that each business will have 15 minutes to produce a prototype of its invention, which will sell for $5.00. As they construct their prototype, the students should complete Activity 9.1, "Calculating Costs of Production." Remind them that to make the most profit, they should keep their costs of production as low as possible, while still creating a product that will be attractive to consumers (their classmates) at a price of $5.00.

6. Using Visual 9.1, demonstrate to the students how to complete Activity 9.1.

   A. Explain that each firm will pay 75 cents in rent for each unit it produces no matter how large the group is or what the group makes.

   B. The amount a firm pays for labor will vary depending on the number of workers in the group: If a firm has four workers, its labor cost will be $1.00 (4 x 25 cents) for each unit it produces.

   C. All other costs depend not only on whether the firm uses a particular resource but also on how much of a resource it uses. You may need to clarify the costs depending on what items you have gathered for the resource bags.

   D. After firms have finished their inventions, they will total the cost of all the resources they used and record this on Activity 9.1. Explain that their total will represent the cost of producing one unit of their product.

7. Give firms about 15 minutes to complete their invention prototypes and Activity 9.1. After they have finished, have a representative from each group give a one-minute sales pitch promoting and demonstrating its invention for the rest of the class. Then line up all the inventions on a table or on desks along one side of the room. You may want to place an envelope in front of each invention to hold the money students will "spend" on it.

8. Explain to the students that they will now role-play consumers. Give each student one play $5.00 bill, and tell them to "buy" their favorite invention. (They may not choose the invention their own group produced). If you use envelopes, the students may proceed group by group to the inventions and deposit their $5.00 in the envelope of the invention they want to purchase. Alternatively, you could have the students raise their hands for their favorite invention as you call out the names of the inventions. Collect the money after each invention is voted on to ensure that each student buys only once.

9. Using Visual 9.2, fill in column 1 (Invention Name) and column 2 (Quantity Sold) for each group. Then have each group calculate its total revenue (which you will enter in column 3) by multiplying the quantity sold by $5.00.

10. Distribute a copy of Activity 9.2, "Calculating Profit," to each of the students. Tell the students to assume that each group will be able to produce all the inventions it "sold" at the same per-unit cost as the prototype.

11. Have the students complete Activity 9.2 using the revenue and cost data for their firm. Discuss the definitions of total revenue, total cost, profit and loss.

12. Call on each firm to report its total cost and profit, and complete columns 4 and 5 on Visual 9.2. Determine which business

had the highest profit. Have the class discuss possible reasons for this group's success. Often the firm with the most sales (column 2) is not the firm with the highest profit because it has higher production costs. Discuss this with the students.

CLOSURE

Discuss the following questions with the class:

1. What resources do producers need to produce goods and services? *Labor, space to work, inputs. The categories economists use are natural resources, human resources (including labor and entrepreneurship) and capital resources.*

2. Why must producers carefully consider which resources to buy? *Because resources cost money and can affect profits: The higher the production costs, the more products a company will need to sell to cover total costs.*

3. What is profit? *Profit is total revenue minus total cost.*

4. Why is profit important to producers? *It determines whether the producer can continue producing, provides a monetary reward to the producer and serves as an incentive for entrepreneurs to accept the risks of business in order to provide consumers with new goods and services.*

5. How are the costs of production passed on to consumers? *The selling price includes the costs of production plus money for profit.*

6. Why do some firms experience losses? *Answers will vary but may include low quantities demanded due to consumer preferences and/or high costs of production.*

7. What eventually happens to a business if no one wants to buy its products? *It will go out of business.*

VISUAL 9.1
CALCULATING COSTS OF PRODUCTION

Company Name	Invention Name

Directions

In column 1, list each resource your business group used to produce your invention.

In column 2, write the price for each unit, using the Resource Price List.

In column 3, write the number of units of each resource your group used.

(For labor, write the number of people in your company.)

In column 4, calculate the total cost of each resource by multiplying column 2 by column 3.

Total the amounts in column 4 to find the cost of producing one unit of your invention.

Write your total in the bottom row of the table.

1. Resource	2. Resource Price per Unit	3. Number of Units Used	4. Total Resource Cost *(column 2 x column 3)*
Rent	$ 0.75	1	$ 0.75
Labor	$ 0.25		
Invention Cost (cost of producing one unit)			

VISUAL 9.2
INVENTION TABLE

1. Invention Name	2. Quantity Sold	3. Total Revenue	4. Total Cost	5. Profit / Loss

ACTIVITY 9.1
CALCULATING COSTS OF PRODUCTION

Company Name	Invention Name

Directions

In column 1, list each resource your business group used to produce your invention.

In column 2, write the price for each unit, using the Resource Price List.

In column 3, write the number of units of each resource your group used.

(For labor, write the number of people in your company.)

In column 4, calculate the total cost of each resource by multiplying column 2 by column 3.

Total the amounts in column 4 to find the cost of producing one unit of your invention.

Write your total in the bottom row of the table.

1. Resource	2. Resource Price per Unit	3. Number of Units Used	4. Total Resource Cost (column 2 x column 3)
Rent	$ 0.75	1	$ 0.75
Labor	$ 0.25		
Invention Cost (cost of producing one unit)			

ACTIVITY 9.2
CALCULATING PROFIT

Company Name	Invention Name

1. The selling price of your company's invention is	**$5.00**

2. How many units did you sell?	

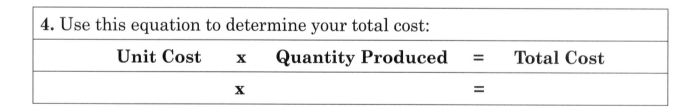

3. Use this equation to determine your total revenue:

Selling Price	x	Quantity Sold	=	Total Revenue
	x		=	

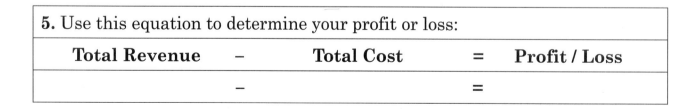

4. Use this equation to determine your total cost:

Unit Cost	x	Quantity Produced	=	Total Cost
	x		=	

5. Use this equation to determine your profit or loss:

Total Revenue	–	Total Cost	=	Profit / Loss
	–		=	

ACTIVITY 9.3
$5.00 BILLS

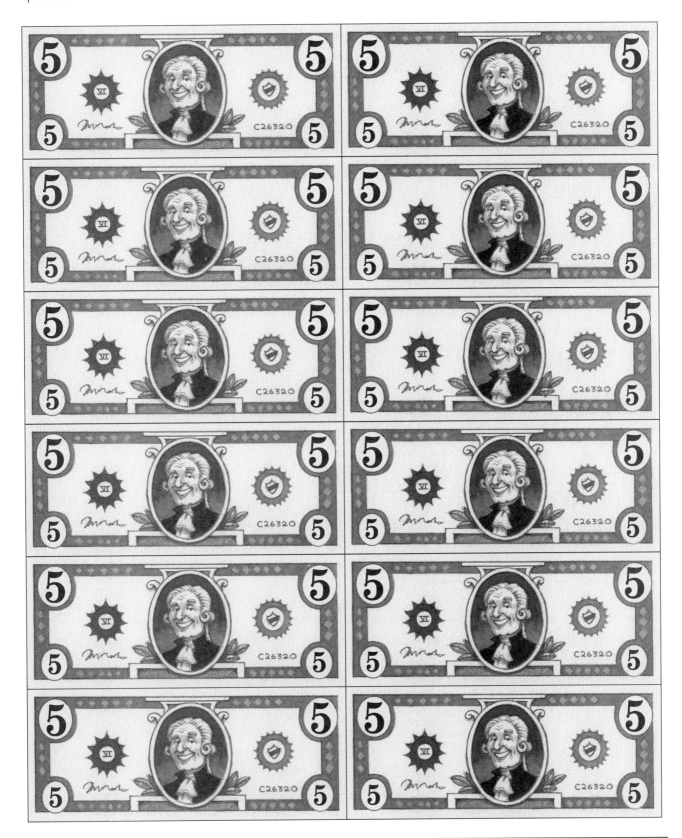

ECONOMICS IN ACTION, © NATIONAL COUNCIL ON ECONOMIC EDUCATION, NEW YORK, N.Y.

Lesson 10 - The Circular Flow of Economic Activity

INTRODUCTION

Economics

The *circular flow of economic activity* is a simplified macroeconomic model of the basic economic relationships in a market economy. This model gives the students an overview of how households, businesses and government interact in different markets by exchanging goods and services, productive resources (also known as *inputs* or the *factors of production*) and money.

Reasoning

People respond to incentives. Households have incentives to provide resources to businesses to receive income in return. They then have incentives to use their income to purchase goods and services to satisfy their wants. Businesses have incentives to earn profits and, therefore, to produce the goods and services that consumers want. To produce goods and services, businesses need to purchase resources from households. The circular-flow model and the simulation in this lesson demonstrate these important relationships.

CONCEPTS

Circular flow of goods, services, productive resources and money payments
Interdependence
Productive resources
   (natural, human and capital)
Resource payments
   (wages and salaries, rent, interest, profit)

CONTENT STANDARDS

7. Markets exist when buyers and sellers interact. This interaction determines market prices and thereby allocates scarce goods and services.

16. There is an economic role for government to play in a market economy whenever the benefits of a government policy outweigh its costs. Governments often provide for national defense, address environmental concerns, define and protect property rights, and attempt to make markets more competitive. Most government policies also redistribute income.

18. A nation's overall levels of income, employment and prices are determined by the interaction of spending and production decisions made by all households, firms, government agencies and others in the economy.

OBJECTIVES

Students will
1. Identify and describe the three types of productive resources (inputs) and the kind of income each resource earns.

2. Analyze the economic relationships between households and businesses in a market economy.

3. Use a circular-flow diagram to illustrate the economic relationships among households, businesses and government.

LESSON DESCRIPTION

In this lesson, the students read about market interactions and participate in a simulation. "Econoland" involves transactions between businesses and households in two kinds of markets: *product* markets and *resource* (or input) markets. They discuss how the government fits into this model and translate their conclusions into a circular-flow diagram.

TIME REQUIRED

75 minutes: 45 minutes to conduct and discuss the simulation and 30 minutes to complete Activities 10.5 and 10.6

MATERIALS

Note: Prepare materials for the simulation before class, mainly cutting apart activity sheets and creating sets of materials for the students. If possible, laminate badges, cards and money to use in multiple classes.

1. Visuals 10.1 and 10.2

2. A copy of Activity 10.1 (two pages) for each student

3. Enough copies of Activity 10.2 (one Business Badge and 10 $100 bills) for half the students in the class. These students will represent businesses.

4. Enough copies of Activity 10.3 (five Human Resources cards, five Natural Resources cards and five Capital Goods cards) for the rest of the students in the class, who will represent households. Mix the sets up so the cards are not distributed equally: Make one set with 15 Natural Resources cards, for example, and another with 10 Human Resources cards and five Capital Goods cards. Just make sure each set includes a total of 15 cards.

5. Enough copies of Activity 10.4 (10 Econo cards) for half the students in the class. You will need to cut these cards apart, but they don't need to be put into sets. Econos will be distributed during the simulation,

so you can put them in an envelope or container to make it easy to give them out.

6. A copy of Activity 10.5 and Activity 10.6 for each student

7. A large piece of paper on which you have written ECONO FACTORY

8. Masking tape or straight pins so the students can wear the Business Badges

9. **(Optional)** Two small prizes

PROCEDURE

1. Explain to the students that people participate in the economy in a variety of ways. People make decisions as consumers when they purchase goods and services. They make decisions as producers when they provide human and natural resources they own to businesses or when their savings allow businesses to borrow to make investments in capital goods. They also make decisions as citizens, especially as voters, that influence the economic decisions made collectively in the economy.

2. Explain that the class will engage in a simulation called "Econoland" to learn about the interrelationships between households and businesses in a market economy.

3. Give each student a copy of Activity 10.1. Instruct the students to read "Overview." Review the role of households, the three categories of productive resources and the roles of business firms. Answer any questions about the concepts involved.

4. Divide the class in half. Students in one group will represent business firms and students in the other group will represent households. Give each business firm 10 $100 bills and a Business Badge to wear during the simulation. Have business firms tape or pin their badges to their shirts to make them more recognizable to the households. Give each household a set of 15 resources cards.

5. Have the students read the instructions for the "Econoland" simulation on the second page of Activity 10.1. Make sure households know they must sell their resources cards for money and then use the money to buy Econos, which represent products. Make sure businesses know they must pay money for the resources cards and then sell Econos to the households.

6. Tape the ECONO FACTORY sign in the place where firms will exchange three cards – one Natural Resources, one Human Resources and one Capital Goods – for one Econo. Remind the students that Econos represent goods and services businesses sell to households. You or a student you select will staff the Econo Factory.

7. Review the instructions for the simulation and answer any questions. Remind the students that the goal of each business firm is to end the simulation with as much money as possible. Businesses must pay money to obtain the productive-resources cards. The goal of each household is to end with as many Econos as possible. Households must sell their resources cards for money, and they may buy only Econos with money.

8. Conduct the simulation. Allow the students up to 20 minutes to engage in their exchange activities (they usually finish in 15 minutes or less). When you observe that about half the households have sold all their resources cards, announce that exchanges will end in five minutes. Students must know in advance when the exchange period will end so they can plan for the orderly sale of their remaining productive resources and Econos. (Some households might try to circumvent the business process by bringing resources cards directly to the Econo Factory. Explain that they lack a Business Badge and therefore cannot produce Econos. If a student is staffing the Econo Factory, make sure the student is aware of this possibility and knows how to respond.)

9. After the simulation ends and the students have returned to their seats, ask them how well they did: Which household obtained the most goods and services (Econos) during the simulation? Which business firm now has the most money? **(Optional)** Provide a small prize to the household with the most Econos and to the business with the most money.

10. Project Visual 10.1. Explain that the diagram shows the circular flow of productive resources (factors of production), goods and services (products) and money payments. Ask the students to describe how households and businesses are interdependent. Ask them to relate the circular-flow diagram on Visual 10.1 to the "Econoland" simulation. *Students who represented businesses acquired productive resources (human-resources, natural-resources and capital-goods cards) from households through the Resource Market in exchange for money-income payments. Businesses exchanged resources cards for Econos, which represent goods and services. Businesses sold Econos to households through the Product Market in exchange for money payments.*

11. Distribute a copy of Activity 10.5 to each student. Tell the students to answer Questions 1, 2 and 3 using the information they gained from the simulation and from Visual 10.1 (reproduced at the top of Activity 10.5). Discuss their answers to the questions.

    1. According to the diagram, in which markets do businesses give money-income payments to households in exchange for their productive resources? *Resource markets*

    2. In which markets do households give money payments to businesses in exchange for goods and services? *Product markets*

    3. What did Econos represent in the simulation? *Goods and services businesses sell to households*

12. Project Visual 10.2, and ask the students to compare this diagram with the diagram on Activity 10.5. Discuss all the ways the circular-flow model was altered to incorporate the government sector and suggest that even more changes would have to be made to the chart if we were to incorporate international-trade relationships.

13. Distribute Activity 10.6 and note that the circular-flow diagram from Visual 10.2 is reproduced at the top. Instruct the students to answer Questions 1, 2, 3 and 4 using the information on Activity 10.6. Discuss the answers.

    1. Give an example of a productive resource that households sell to government. *Answers will vary and include teachers working in public schools.*

    2. Give an example of a good or service that businesses sell to government.

Answers will vary and include computers, communications satellites, accounting services and airplanes.

    3. Give an example of a good or service that government provides to households in exchange for money payments, mainly taxes. *Answers will vary and include schools, police and fire departments, roads and libraries.*

    4. Give an example of a good or service that government provides to businesses in exchange for money payments. *Answers will vary and include police, highways, air-traffic control services and disaster assistance.*

Note: *Transfer payments* are government payments for which recipients do not currently perform productive services. Significant transfer payments in the United States today include Social Security benefits, Medicare and Medicaid, government-employee retirement benefits, unemployment compensation and public assistance such as food stamps.

CLOSURE

Explain to the class that the U.S. economy is organized around a system of private markets in which prices for goods and services are determined by the interaction of buyers and sellers. This form of economic activity creates a type of interdependence between people in households and people in businesses. Ask:

1. How do individuals and families in households depend on people in businesses?

People in households buy the goods and services they desire from businesses. They sell the productive resources they own to businesses to earn income.

2. How do businesses depend on individuals and families in households?

Businesses sell goods and services to households to earn revenue and make a profit. They purchase productive resources from households to produce the goods and services consumers desire.

3. What is the role of government in the circular flow of economic activity?

Government taxes businesses and households to pay for the productive resources it uses to provide certain kinds of goods and services to households and businesses.

VISUAL 10.1
THE CIRCULAR FLOW OF PRODUCTIVE RESOURCES, GOODS AND SERVICES AND MONEY PAYMENTS

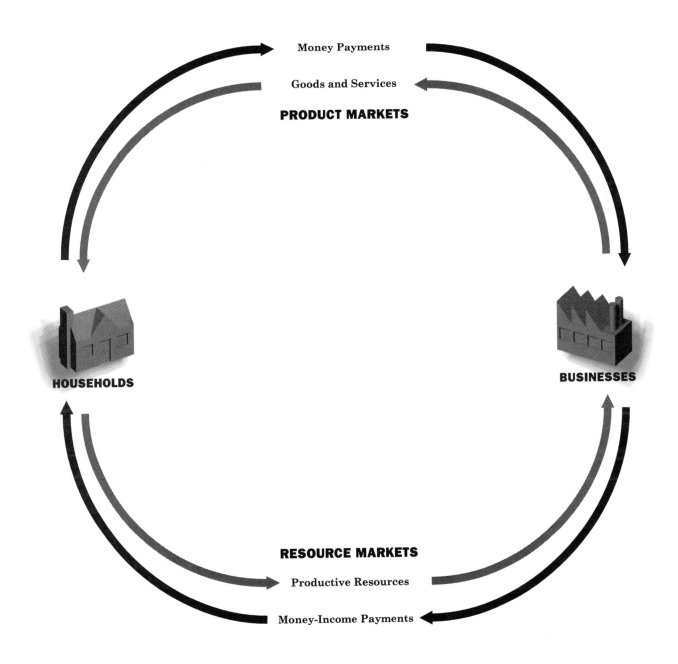

VISUAL 10.2
GOVERNMENT IN THE CIRCULAR FLOW

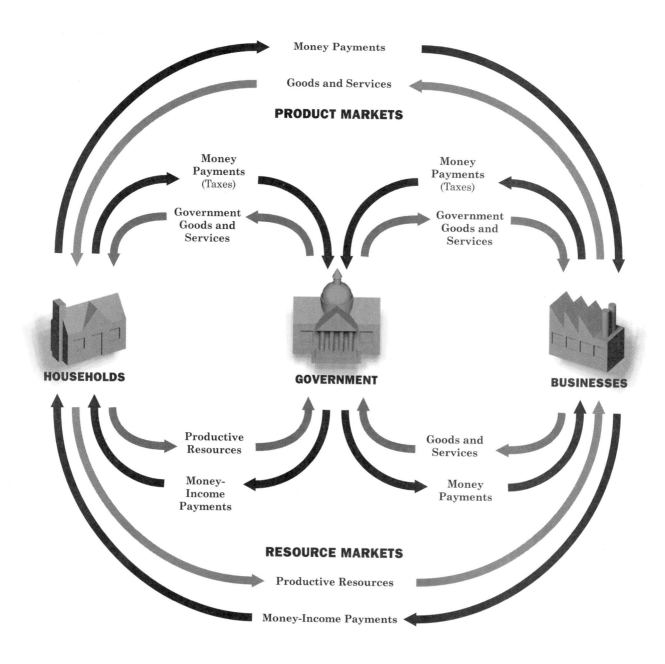

Money Payments

Goods and Services

PRODUCT MARKETS

Money
Payments
(Taxes)

Money
Payments
(Taxes)

Government
Goods and
Services

Government
Goods and
Services

HOUSEHOLDS

GOVERNMENT

BUSINESSES

Productive
Resources

Goods and
Services

Money-
Income
Payments

Money
Payments

RESOURCE MARKETS

Productive Resources

Money-Income Payments

ACTIVITY 10.1
EARNING A LIVING IN ECONOLAND

OVERVIEW

The Roles of Households (Individuals and Families)

Individuals function as both consumers and producers. In the U.S. economy, households act as consumers when they buy goods and services that businesses produce. These exchanges take place in *product markets*. Buying food at a local grocery store is an exchange in a product market.

As resource owners, individuals function as producers by supplying productive resources to businesses, which use these resources to produce goods and services. These exchanges take place in *resource markets* (also called *factor, productive-resource* or *input markets*). Examples of transactions that occur in resource markets are businesses paying wages to workers, rent to landowners or interest on loans for plant and equipment.

Businesses use three categories of productive resources to produce goods and services: human resources, natural resources and capital.

> **Human resources** are the number of people available for work and the skills and motivation of these individuals. Businesses pay wages and salaries to households for their labor services. *Entrepreneurship* refers to a special type of human resource that assumes the risk of organizing other resources to produce goods and services. The payment to entrepreneurs is called *profit*.

> **Natural resources** are gifts of nature. These include undeveloped land, oceans and rivers, forests, oil and mineral deposits, and climactic conditions.

> **Capital** refers to the manufactured or constructed items that businesses use in the production process. These items include buildings, machinery and equipment. (In everyday speech, people commonly refer to money as capital; but in economics, the term *capital* refers to the real productive resources used to produce other goods and services.)

The Roles of Business Firms

Like households, businesses function as both consumers and producers. Businesses supply goods and services in the product market. They are the buyers, or consumers, of the productive resources (human resources, natural resources and capital resources) used to produce goods and services. Businesses try to sell their products for more than their costs of production, thereby earning a profit. If a business is not successful, it will incur losses. In order to earn a profit, businesses must supply products that households want to buy and supply these products at competitive prices. If a business doesn't produce what households want to buy, or if it doesn't keep its costs of production low enough to compete with other producers, it will incur losses. A firm will eventually go out of business if it continues to incur losses.

ACTIVITY 10.1, continued
EARNING A LIVING IN ECONOLAND

INSTRUCTIONS FOR THE ECONOLAND SIMULATION

In this simulation, you will play the role of either a household or a business. Read carefully about both roles. Then your teacher will assign your role.

Households:

Your first goal is to sell to businesses the human resources, natural resources and capital goods they use to produce a product. Then, with the income you earn from selling those productive resources, you will purchase from businesses the goods and services your household wants to consume. In this simulation, these goods and services are called Econos. Your success as a household will be measured by the number of Econos you accumulate. You will be given 15 Productive Resource cards. You may not want to sell all your resources immediately because their prices may change as the game goes on. In general, however, the more resources you sell, the more money you will earn to acquire Econos. Be sure to sell all your resource cards before the activity ends, because at the end of the simulation, only the Econos you have will count.

Business Firms:

Your goal is to earn a profit by supplying the goods and services households want. In this activity, the only products households want to buy are Econos. To produce one Econo, you must acquire one unit of human resources, one unit of natural resources and one unit of capital goods. You must buy these resources from households at the best price you can negotiate. Once you have accumulated one unit of each resource, you may turn the set of three cards in at the Econo Factory, which will produce one Econo for you. You are then free to sell the Econo to any household for the best price you can negotiate. To earn a profit, you must sell the Econo for more than your costs of production, which in this game include the wages and salaries paid for the use of human resources, the rent paid for the use of natural resources and the interest paid for the use of capital. You can then use the money you receive to buy more productive resources in order to produce and sell more Econos. You have $1,000 to start the game. Your business success will be measured by the dollars you have at the end of the activity. Try to sell all your Econos by the end of the activity. If you run out of money and have no Econos to sell, announce publicly that you are bankrupt and return to your seat.

A Word about Pricing:

You will use only $100 bills in this activity. It is possible to arrive at prices other than $100, $200, $300, etc., by combining several items in a single transaction. For example, two Productive Resources cards could be sold for $300, which is the equivalent of $150 each. Five cards could be sold for $300, which is the equivalent of $60 each. However, you must agree on a price for which an exchange can take place using the denominations of money provided in the simulation. The suggested price range for Productive Resources cards is $50 to $300, but any price that buyers and sellers agree to and can complete using $100 bills is acceptable.

ACTIVITY 10.2
BUSINESS BADGE AND MONEY

BUSINESS

ACTIVITY 10.3
HOUSEHOLD CARDS

ACTIVITY 10.4
ECONO CARDS

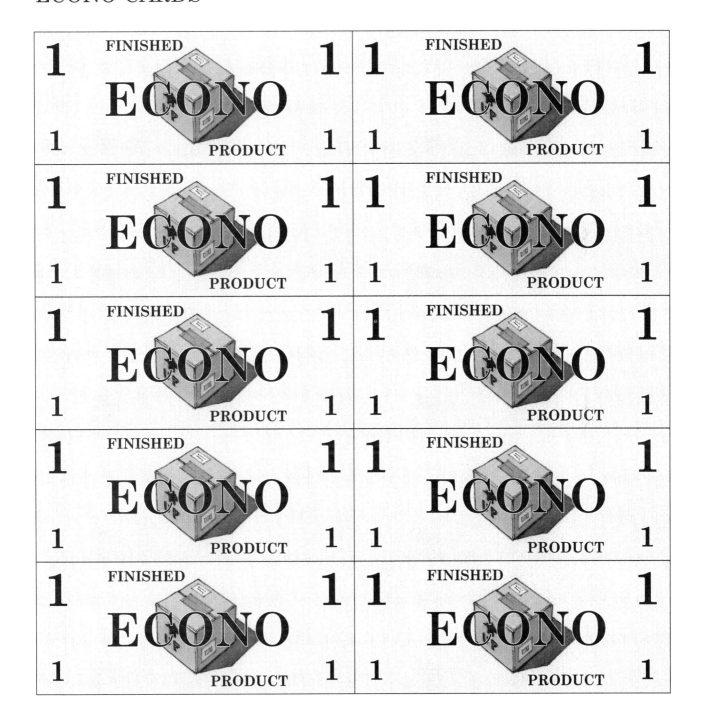

ACTIVITY 10.5
THE CIRCULAR FLOW OF PRODUCTIVE RESOURCES, GOODS AND SERVICES AND MONEY PAYMENTS

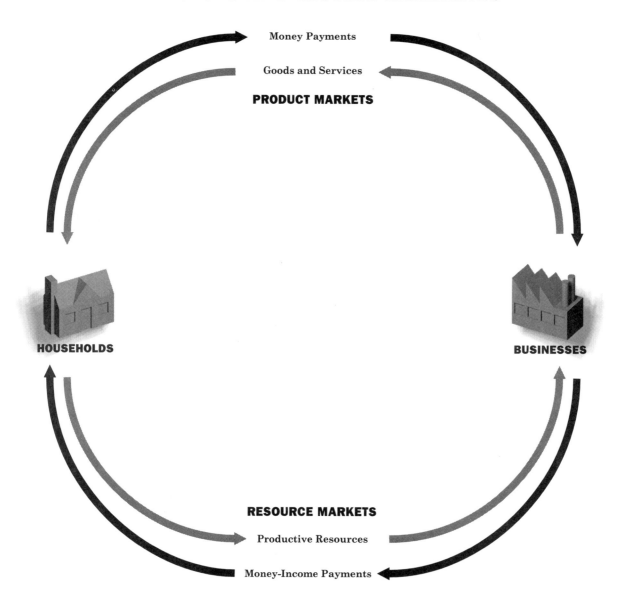

1. According to the diagram, in which markets do businesses give money-income payments to households in exchange for their productive resources?

2. In which markets do households give money payments to businesses in exchange for goods and services?

3. What did Econos represent in the simulation?

ACTIVITY 10.6
GOVERNMENT IN THE CIRCULAR FLOW

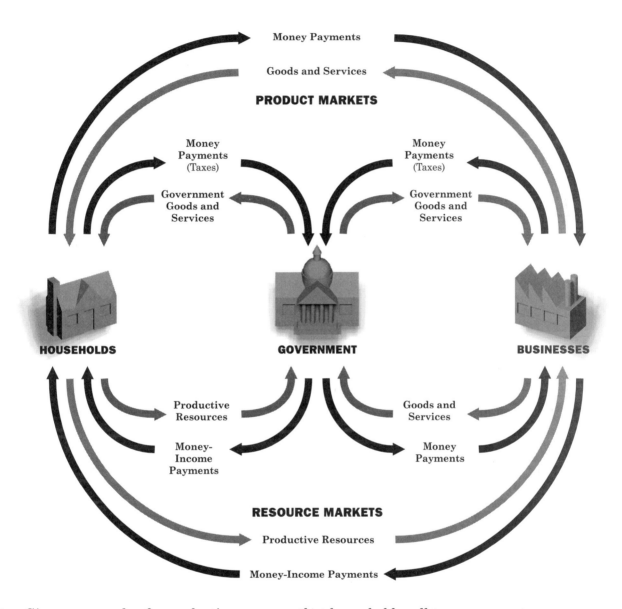

1. Give an example of a productive resource that households sell to government.

2. Give an example of a good or service that businesses sell to government.

3. Give an example of a good or service that government provides to households in exchange for money payments, mainly taxes.

4. Give an example of a good or service that government provides to businesses in exchange for money payments.

Lesson 11 - Money and Inflation

INTRODUCTION

Economics

Many people think economics is the study of money. In fact, economics is much more than this; however, money is an important tool of the exchange process and helps the economy run. Money makes it easier and more efficient for people to transfer ownership of goods and services.

The supply of money in the economy is a very important macroeconomic variable. When the total amount of money in the economy changes or when people's incomes change, behavior in the marketplace changes. The basic cause of *inflation* is an increase in the rate of growth of the money supply relative to the rate of growth of goods and services. The Federal Reserve System, the nation's central bank, has the responsibility of managing the U.S. money supply.

Reasoning

A key assumption of economic reasoning is that people respond to incentives in predictable ways. This assumption relates to both the use of money and the underlying cause of inflation. Money offers an incentive for many people because it represents potential ownership of things of value. In addition, prices, expressed in terms of money, help people easily understand the relative value of things. When the money supply is growing faster than the supply of goods and services in an economy, people have incentives to spend money before prices go up. This causes inflation and leads to *inflationary spirals*.

CONCEPTS

Federal Reserve System
Functions of money
Inflation
Monetary policy
Money
MV = PQ

CONTENT STANDARDS

11. Money makes it easier to trade, borrow, save, invest and compare the value of goods and services.

19. Unexpected inflation imposes costs on many people and benefits some others because it arbitrarily redistributes purchasing power. Inflation can reduce the rate of growth of national living standards, because individuals and organizations use resources to protect themselves against the uncertainty of future prices.

20. Federal government budgetary policy and the Federal Reserve System's monetary policy influence the overall levels of employment, output and prices.

OBJECTIVES

Students will
1. Observe a demonstration to understand the functions of money.

2. Participate in an auction to determine the monetary cause of inflation.

3. Use the equation MV = PQ to understand the relationship among the money supply, the price level, the velocity of money and real output.

LESSON DESCRIPTION

Students observe a simple demonstration to determine the functions that money performs. They next participate in two rounds of an auction illustrating how increases in the money supply lead to inflation. They view an active demonstration of the equation MV = PQ to understand the relationship among the variables and the intent of monetary policy. This lesson may be used as either an introduction to or a review of monetary policy and the role of the Federal Reserve System. The three activities may be done separately or together.

TIME REQUIRED

60 minutes

MATERIALS

1. Visuals 11.1, 11.2 and 11.3

2. Three pieces of paper (could be pages torn from magazines) and a dollar bill. Make sure at least one piece of paper is larger or more colorful than the dollar.

3. A supply of white beans and black beans (or play money) to use as money

4. Two each of three desirable products to be auctioned off such as pencils or candy bars **(Optional)** Two copies each of three pictures cut from magazines that show a consumer good such as houses or cars. These pictures will represent items being auctioned.

5. Five large sheets of colored paper or cardboard with one of the following written on each: M, V, =, P, Q

PROCEDURE

1. Hold up and inspect three pieces of paper and a dollar bill. Comment on how they are alike and different. For example, you may comment on the size, colors, pictures, etc. Do not refer to the dollar as money; just talk about it as another piece of paper. Then announce you have decided you don't have time for this lesson. Crumple the pieces of paper and the dollar and throw them on a desk or the floor. Ask a nearby student to throw them in the wastepaper basket for you. Watch the student carefully to see if he or she hesitates

to throw away the dollar, which will probably occur. Say nothing until the student makes a decision about what to do with the dollar bill. Then ask the student to explain his or her response to your request. Ask the class what they would decide to do with the dollar and why. *Answers will vary but will likely include possible uses for the dollar (spending or saving) or comments about how the dollar has value, while the crumpled papers do not.*

2. Ask the students what makes a dollar different from the other pieces of paper. List their answers on the board. Display Visual 11.1 to illustrate the functions of money as a medium of exchange, a store of value and a measure of value. Discuss these functions, and compare with the list generated by the students.

3. Tell the students that you will further explore the role of money in the economy by conducting two auctions. Show the class two identical sets of three valuable products to be auctioned off separately in two rounds. These goods represent total output in your classroom economy during two time periods. Quickly distribute a few white beans in varying amounts to each student. Tell the students each bean is worth $1. You will auction the products to the highest bidders. Students may ask if they may combine beans and bid with other students. It is fine to permit this, but it can greatly draw out the time spent on the auction. To keep the activity relatively short, tell the students the auction will go quickly, and you will stop accepting bids at your discretion.
(Optional) Show the students the two sets of pictures and tell them they will engage in a simulated auction for the items in the pictures. This method of handling the auction is particularly effective if your school is in an area with high housing prices and you use pictures of single-family homes or condos. If you use this option, you may want to make the bidding

more realistic by telling the students that each bean or piece of play money represents $10,000 instead of $1.00.

4. Conduct the auction for the first item. Collect the beans the students spent. Record the selling price on the board. Conduct the auctions for the second and third items and collect the beans. Ask the students to discuss what occurred.

5. Pass out a supply of black beans for the second round of auctions, and announce that they are worth $5 each (or $50,000 each if you are simulating a home or car auction). Anyone who still has white beans may use them in the second round. Quickly conduct the auctions for the three products, which should be identical to the items auctioned in the first round. Collect the beans and record the prices on the board. The second set of prices should be considerably higher than the first. Let the bidding for each good go on long enough to make sure this happens. Ask the students to discuss what occurred. Emphasize that you auctioned the same products each time. Why were the prices higher in the second auction? *Answers will vary. Students may comment that they knew they were bidding for the last item available, and therefore knew their beans would have no value after the item was auctioned off. Someone should mention that there was more money available for people to spend in the second round, and this resulted in higher prices.*

6. Define inflation as *a sustained increase in the average price level of all of the goods and services produced in the economy.* Point out that in market economies, some prices are always changing because of supply and demand. For example, if the price of strawberries or snowboards goes up, this does not mean there is inflation. Inflation occurs when there is an increase in the average of all prices. The fundamental underlying cause of inflation was demonstrated in the auctions: When the money supply in an economy increases relative to the supply of goods and services, the overall level of prices generally increases.

7. Tell the students they will participate in an activity to further emphasize and illustrate the relationship between the money supply and inflation. Ask for five volunteers to come to the front of the room and hold a sign. Give each student one of the M, V, = , P and Q cards. Line the volunteers up facing the class across the front of the room in this order: MV = PQ. This is known as the *equation of exchange*.

8. Display Visual 11.2 and discuss the definitions of the variables. First, tell the volunteer holding the equal sign that he or she has the easiest job: Just stand there. Tell the other volunteers they will be the stars of the show; they should wave their signs as the respective definition is read. Tell the class that this simple equation is a model of the macro economy: MV represents the demand side and PQ represents the supply side. Remind the students of a rule of basic algebra: If one side of an equation goes up, something must also go up on the other side of the equation to keep the two sides equal.

9. Ask all the volunteers except the equal sign to do a deep knee bend.
   A. Tell M to stand up – to indicate an increase in the money supply.
   B. Ask P what he or she should do if Q and V do not change. *Stand up.* Why? *An increase in the money supply will mean an increase in the price level if nothing else changes.*
   C. Ask the students to do a deep knee bend again.
   D. Tell the students that the velocity of money may decrease during recessions because people are afraid to spend too much money. It may increase during inflation as people try to beat price increases.
   E. Tell V to rise and tell M and Q to

stay the same. What happens to P? *It rises.* Tell V to do a deep knee bend. What happens to P? *It should do a deep knee bend, too.* You could have V and P do a dance – up, up, down, down.

F. Ask the students to do another deep knee bend.

G. Ask M to move up a little. Have Q move up to the same level. V should stay the same.

H. Ask P what he or she should do now. *Stay put, because M and Q are in balance.*

10. Discuss what the five students have demonstrated.

A. What happens to prices if you increase the money supply, and both the quantity of goods and services and the velocity of money do not increase? *Prices rise; there is inflation.*

B. What happens to prices if the money supply and the quantity of goods and services stay the same but the velocity of money increases? *Prices rise; there is inflation.*

C. Monetarists believe you can predict changes in the velocity of money. Other economists disagree. What difference does it make whether you can predict changes in the velocity of money? *If V is predictable, it is possible to control inflation by controlling the money supply.*

D. What happens to prices if the quantity of goods and services increases and the money supply increases by the same amount? *Prices do not change; there is no inflation.*

11. Now relate the simulation to the actions of the Federal Reserve System. The Fed is the central banking system in the United States. One of its primary jobs is to engage in monetary policy to try to control the nation's money supply. The Fed's purpose is to prevent inflation and declines in real output, which could lead to recession and unemployment.

A. In a period of inflation (when the price level has increased), what should the

Fed do to lower prices? *Lower the money supply*

B. In a period of recession, unemployment is high and the amount of goods and services has decreased. What should the Fed do to increase the production of goods and services? *Increase the money supply.* The students may ask why inflation wouldn't occur as in Question 10A. It may happen; however, the difference here is that the supply of goods and services can change, while in A it couldn't. Refer to Question 10D to illustrate this.

12. **(Optional)** Instruct the students to act out these additional examples as you read them, following your instructions.

A. Many economists believe there was a monetary cause of the Great Depression in the United States: It is well known that the output of goods and services fell dramatically between 1929 and 1933 (ask Q to do a deep knee bend), and many causes are often cited for this. An important point is that the Fed dramatically decreased the money supply between 1930 and 1933 (M should do a deep knee bend), and this may have led to the declines in output. There is also some evidence that velocity decreased as well (V should join M and Q in a deep knee bend): Because people didn't trust banks, they were hoarding money and not spending it as fast. Prices also fell dramatically during this period (P should do a deep knee bend).

B. Economists distinguish between real values and nominal values. We can use the MV = PQ equation to illustrate the difference between real GDP and nominal GDP. Real GDP is defined as GDP adjusted for inflation, or measured in terms of constant purchasing power. In this equation, Q represents real GDP. Nominal GDP means GDP measured in current dollars, or not adjusted for inflation. In this equation, PQ represents nominal GDP. Ask all the students to do a deep knee bend. Then tell the class that the intent of monetary policy in a recession is to increase the money supply (ask M to rise) to increase real GDP (Q should rise). However, many economists believe that in the long run, these increases in the money supply lead only to inflation (P should rise).

C. If the students ask about the behavior of velocity, you may want to explain that economists once believed velocity was relatively constant and stable and was represented by a number such as four. However, from the mid-1950s to the early 1980s, the most common measure of velocity increased from about three to more than seven in the United States. Since then it has fluctuated between six and seven. If velocity is unpredictable, this can greatly offset the effects of monetary policy. You can show this with $MV = PQ$. Ask all the students to stand if they aren't already. Assume the Fed decreases M (M should do a deep knee bend) to try to decrease P (P should do a deep knee bend). However if V increases (V should raise the card over his or her head), the decrease in the money supply may not cause a decrease in P (P should return to his or her original position), and monetary policy may be ineffective.

CLOSURE

Display Visual 11.3 and review the definitions of inflation, the Federal Reserve and monetary policy. Review the results of the auction activity and why the money supply in the economy is important. (If you use this lesson as an introduction to monetary policy, you may want to follow it up by having the students discuss the tools of monetary policy. If you use this lesson as a review of monetary policy, the students may review how the specific tools of monetary policy lead to increases or decreases in the money supply.)

VISUAL 11.1
FUNCTIONS OF MONEY

What Makes Money Important?

Money serves these functions:

1. **It is a medium of exchange.**
   Money is valuable because it is accepted in buying and selling goods and services. Money makes trading easier than would be the case with barter.

2. **It is a store of value.**
   Money is a way of storing wealth. For example, if you work today, you can get paid in money and wait to spend it in the future.

3. **It is a measure of value.**
   Money can be used to state how much things are worth. The value of goods and services can be expressed in money prices, allowing for easy comparisons.

VISUAL 11.2
MV=PQ

M: the supply of money in the economy

V: the velocity of money, or the number of times a year that the average dollar is spent on final goods and services

P: the overall price level in the economy, reflecting the average price at which all output is sold

Q: the quantity of all goods and services produced; also known as *real* output

The equation MV = PQ is a simple model of a macro economy during a time period. MV represents the total amount spent by buyers in the economy, and PQ represents the total amount received by sellers, so the two must be equal. If there is a change in one of the variables, there must be a change in one of the other variables to keep MV equal to PQ.

VISUAL 11.3
INFLATION, THE FED AND MONETARY POLICY

Inflation: a sustained increase in the average price level of all the goods and services produced in the economy

Federal Reserve: the central banking system in the United States, often called the Fed. Among other things, the Fed has the job of conducting monetary policy to control the money supply.

Monetary Policy: when a nation's central bank changes the money supply to promote stable prices, full employment and economic growth. Monetary policy tries to address problems of inflation and unemployment.

Why is the money supply in the economy important?

Too much money relative to the supply of goods and services can cause inflation. Too little money can cause decreases in production, leading to unemployment.

Lesson 12 - Fiscal Policy: A Two-Act Play

INTRODUCTION

Economics

The government is often blamed when the economy experiences unemployment, decreasing gross domestic product or inflation. Many economists believe that the federal government can, and should, help alleviate these problems at times by using traditional, discretionary *fiscal policy*.

Traditional (or *demand side*) fiscal policy advocates that in times of recession and above-normal unemployment, the government should deliberately increase spending on goods and services and/or reduce taxes to increase *aggregate demand*. In theory, this has *multiplier effects* and stimulates other spending, which results in increased production and more jobs. In times of inflation, traditional fiscal policy calls for reduced government spending and/or increases in taxes to decrease aggregate demand. Reductions in aggregate demand should then lead to decreased prices.

Traditional fiscal policy has its critics for several reasons. Economists do not know with certainty how large multiplier effects are or how long it takes fiscal policy to work. Therefore, by the time an expansionary fiscal policy takes effect, the economy may no longer be in a recession and the policy may actually lead to inflation. Additionally, events in other countries can greatly affect the outcome of U.S. fiscal-policy measures. Furthermore, most economists recognize the possibility of *crowding out*, which occurs if government borrowing (for example, to finance expansionary fiscal policy) causes interest rates to rise and private investment spending to decrease.

Some economists emphasize the importance of the *supply-side* effects of fiscal policy, particularly with respect to tax cuts: Business tax cuts give businesses more after-tax income to spend as they choose. This would lead to increased production and investment in capital goods, which, in turn, would lead to a direct increase in aggregate supply, lower unemployment and lower inflation.

Reasoning

Economic theory tells us that people respond to incentives in predictable ways. The effectiveness of fiscal policy depends on how people respond to incentives. For example, if you are given a tax cut, will you spend the extra money or save it? If you spend it, it becomes someone else's income; and if they spend their income (and their tax cut), this has a stimulative effect on the economy. However, if everyone saves the tax cut, which may also be rational, the desired effect of the fiscal policy may be much smaller or nonexistent. Issues such as these make it difficult to predict the effects of fiscal policy.

CONCEPTS

Contractionary fiscal policy
Expansionary fiscal policy
Fiscal policy
Multiplier effects
Supply-side fiscal policy
(Optional) Crowding out

CONTENT STANDARDS

12. Interest rates, adjusted for inflation, rise and fall to balance the amount saved with the amount borrowed, thus affecting the allocation of scarce resources between present and future uses.

20. Federal government budgetary policy and the Federal Reserve System's monetary policy influence the overall levels of employment, output and prices.

OBJECTIVES

Students will
1. Create and act in a play that demonstrates the effects of expansionary and contractionary fiscal policies.

2. Apply fiscal-policy concepts to the situations in the play.

3. **(Optional)** Discuss current debates about the effectiveness of fiscal policy.

LESSON DESCRIPTION

Groups of students are given outlines for one of two acts in a play describing either expansionary or contractionary fiscal policy. After the students choose parts and prepare lines for their roles, two groups are chosen to perform the play. Students then discuss the events in the play using a Visual that defines concepts related to fiscal policy. More advanced classes may then discuss current debates about the effectiveness of fiscal policy.

TIME REQUIRED

60 to 75 minutes

MATERIALS

1. Visual 12.1

2. A copy of Activity 12.1 for half the students in the class

3. A copy of Activity 12.2 for the other half of the class

4. **(Optional)** Visual 12.2

PROCEDURE

1. Tell the students that today they will participate in a two-act play. This play is a little different from others because they have to write their own lines.

2. Divide the students into groups of eight. Pass out a copy of Activity 12.1 (Act 1) to half the groups and a copy of Activity 12.2 (Act 2) to the other half. (If there are fewer than eight students in a group, some students may have more than one part, or the last part before the narrator may be eliminated. They may also add parts if necessary, if you are sure they get the idea.)

3. Read through the directions for the Activities with students (the directions are the same for both acts). Announce that they will have about 15 minutes to prepare their act. After the groups have finished, you will choose one group to perform each act to the class. Encourage the students to be creative, but tell them that they must follow the ideas in the script. Emphasize that each act should take about ten minutes or less to perform, so each character should say only a few sentences. Students will perform the play by lining up in front of the class in order (one through eight) and delivering their lines to the person standing next to them, so they won't need to walk back and forth. (If you do not impose these restrictions and time limits, some students tend to get very carried away with their roles!)

4. Have the students work in their groups. Circulate among the groups to answer questions. You may want to give examples to help some groups get started. When most groups are close to finishing, announce that three minutes remain before the curtain rises.

5. Select one group to come to the front of the room to perform Act 1. When this group has finished, give them a round of applause and tell the students that you will discuss the economic events after Act 2. Select a group to perform Act 2, and give them a round of applause when they have finished. Ask all the students to return to their seats. You may want to explain that according to economic theory, Act 2 does not necessarily follow directly from Act 1. In other words, demand-pull inflation is not always an immediate result of expansionary fiscal policy, although it may occur in the long run. The play was written with the same characters in each act to show multiplier effects affecting the same people in different ways.

6. Display Visual 12.1. Discuss the play as it relates to the terms. Encourage the students to take notes from the Visual as you discuss the following concepts.

   A. Both acts of the play showed examples of *fiscal policy*.

   B. Act 1 showed a tax decrease – an example of *expansionary fiscal policy* – to help fight the recessionary problems of unemployment and decreasing gross domestic product.

   C. Because the househusband decided to spend his tax cut, this became income to the car salesperson, whose spending became income to the computer salesperson, and so on. This is an example of the *multiplier effect* leading to higher GDP and more jobs.

   D. Act 2 showed a decrease in government spending – an example of *contractionary fiscal policy* – to help fight inflation. Here the multiplier effect worked in reverse, as the engineer's lower income led to lower demand and lower prices.

   E. Supply-side fiscal policy is displayed in Act 1 when the restaurant owner uses the tax cut to expand the business, thus creating jobs for people who build the new restaurants and, in turn, boosting GDP.

7. **(Optional)** Tell the students that fiscal policy is controversial and has its critics. Economists disagree about how well it works. For example, what if people in Act 1 decided to save their tax cuts instead of spending them? *This might have limited or eliminated the expansionary effect of the tax cut.* Display Visual 12.2. Use the Visual to discuss the issues surrounding the effectiveness of fiscal policy. (Although these issues are covered in most high-school textbooks, they are somewhat complex and you may wish to reserve this discussion for more advanced classes.)

CLOSURE

To test how well the students understand the desired effects of expansionary and contractionary fiscal policy, assign them to write another act for the Fiscal Policy Play. The additional act could be "Expansionary Fiscal Policy: The Increase in Government Spending" or "Contractionary Fiscal Policy: The Tax Increase." Choose the best acts turned in, and give groups extra credit for performing them for the class.

VISUAL 12.1
FISCAL POLICY TERMS

Fiscal Policy: changes in federal-government spending or taxes designed to promote full employment, price stability and reasonable rates of economic growth

Expansionary Fiscal Policy: an increase in government spending and/or a decrease in taxes designed to increase aggregate demand in the economy. The intent is to increase gross domestic product and reduce unemployment.

Contractionary Fiscal Policy: a decrease in government spending and/or an increase in taxes designed to decrease aggregate demand in the economy. The intent is to control inflation.

Multiplier Effects: in economics, the idea that increased spending by consumers, businesses or government becomes income for someone else. When this person spends the income, it becomes income for someone else and so on, leading to increased production in an economy. Multiplier effects can also work in reverse when spending decreases.

Supply-Side Fiscal Policy: the idea that fiscal policy may directly affect aggregate supply and not just aggregate demand. For example, a tax cut may give businesses incentives to expand or invest in capital goods, since they have more after-tax income to spend as they choose.

VISUAL 12.2
DEBATES ABOUT FISCAL POLICY

1. **How large are the multiplier effects?**
   It is important to know this to decide how large the initial change in taxes and government spending must be to effectively fight recession or inflation. Too large a change could cause more problems, and too small a change would not solve anything. However, economists do not know precisely how large multiplier effects are.

2. **How fast does fiscal policy work?**
   Time lags frequently occur with fiscal policy because of the time it takes
   A. to realize there is a problem in the economy
   B. to get a change in taxes or spending policy passed by Congress
   C. for the fiscal policy to affect the recession or inflation
   Economists cannot predict how long these lags will be and therefore cannot predict how long it will take fiscal policy to help the economy.

3. **How is fiscal policy affected by international events?**
   The U.S. is part of the world economy and is greatly affected by world events it does not control. Actions in other countries may affect how or if U.S. fiscal policy achieves its goals. For example, the U.S. government may try to fight a recession by increasing aggregate demand. But people in other countries may offset this if they decide to buy fewer U.S. exports, decreasing aggregate demand for U.S. goods and services.

4. **How does fiscal policy affect the national debt and interest rates?**
   Since expansionary fiscal policy means government spending goes up or tax revenue goes down, this will most likely boost a current national deficit or cut a current surplus. This may lead to increased interest rates in the economy. When interest rates rise, private businesses may borrow less and slow their investment in capital goods. This *crowding out* of private investment may offset the expansionary effects of fiscal policy.

ACTIVITY 12.1
FISCAL POLICY: A TWO-ACT PLAY – ACT 1

Directions: In your group, choose parts and prepare a few lines to act out your role. To perform the play, you will line up next to each other in order and deliver your lines to the person standing next to you. Make sure you follow the ideas described!

EXPANIONARY FISCAL POLICY: THE TAX CUT

Location: Yourtown, U.S.A.
Time: In the near future, when you are adults in the workforce

Characters and Description of Roles
1. **Narrator/Economist:** Opens Act 1 of the play. Announces that the economy is in a deep recession. Gross domestic product has decreased steadily during the past year, along with consumer spending and business investment. This has resulted in increased unemployment nationwide. People are calling for the government to do something to help the situation.

2. **President of the United States (via radio broadcast):** Announces that the tax cut to households and businesses she (or he) has been promising was approved by the House and Senate and will be put into effect immediately via tax-rebate checks. Tells listeners the recession is, of course, not the fault of her political party; and she firmly believes the tax cut will help to stimulate the economy and create jobs.

3. **Househusband (takes care of the children while his wife works outside the home):** Is delighted to receive the tax-rebate check. Spends the money by putting it toward the down payment on a new car the family desperately needs.

4. **Car Salesperson:** Notes that car sales have picked up, so incomes for car salespeople have increased. Will spend the increased income to buy a new computer for the home.

5. **Computer-store Manager:** Describes how computer sales have increased recently. Needs to hire more workers to handle the additional consumer demand.

6. **Unemployed Computer Technician:** Gets hired at the computer store and is happy to be working again. Celebrates by taking the family out to dinner.

7. **Restaurant Owner:** Discusses how business at the restaurant has increased. The increased revenue, along with the tax cut to businesses, provides the incentive to expand the business by building more restaurants.

8. **Laid-off Construction Worker:** Gets called back to work to build a new restaurant. Will use part of the income from the job to take a trip to Hawaii.

   Narrator/Economist: Closes Act 1. Summarizes effects of tax cut by pointing out that it has encouraged consumer spending and business investment. As individuals and businesses spent more money, more goods and services were produced. GDP increased, and unemployment decreased.

ACTIVITY 12.2
FISCAL POLICY: A TWO-ACT PLAY – ACT 2

Directions: In your group, choose parts and prepare a few lines to act out your role. To perform the play, you will line up next to each other in order and deliver your lines to the person standing next to you. Make sure you follow the ideas described!

CONTRACTIONARY FISCAL POLICY: THE DECREASE IN GOVERNMENT SPENDING

Location: Yourtown, U.S.A.
Time: In the near future, when you are adults in the workforce

Characters and Description of Roles
1. **Narrator/Economist:** Opens Act 2 of the play. Announces that the economy has experienced high and increasing demand-pull inflation for some time. Prices are increasing rapidly. People are calling for the government to do something to help the situation.

2. **President of the United States (via radio broadcast):** Announces that to cure inflation, government will cut spending, in part by decreasing spending on aerospace and other government-funded programs. This will reduce overall demand in the economy and take pressure off rising prices. Tells listeners inflation is, of course, not the fault of her (or his) political party. Firmly believes the decrease in government spending will help to end inflation.

3. **Aerospace Engineer:** Is laid off from government position. Accepts lower-paying position elsewhere. Because of cut in pay, decides not to buy a new home right now.

4. **Construction Worker in Housing Industry:** Notes that sales of new homes have slowed, housing prices are falling and he is working fewer hours. His family can't afford to eat out as often as before.

5. **Restaurant Owner:** Comments that business has fallen, but also notes that supplies are getting cheaper and workers can be hired at lower salaries than before. Decides to cut prices of restaurant meals to get customers to return. Decides not to buy a new computer at this time.

6. **Computer-store Manager:** Discusses how sales are down and inventories are up, but costs of supplies also appear to be falling. Lowers prices on computers in inventory to encourage sales.

7. **Computer Technician:** Because of decreased revenue at computer store, loses overtime pay. Decides not to buy a new car until the prices of new cars fall as much as his pay.

8. **Car Salesperson:** The decline in car prices has reduced her commission on sales. Will tell her husband, who stays home with the kids, to cancel their vacation until the prices fall enough for them to afford it. Notes that overall in the economy, prices are falling.

Narrator/Economist: Closes Act 2. Summarizes effects of government-spending cut by pointing out that it reduced overall demand in the economy, caused prices to fall and slowed the rate of inflation. As spending decreased, incomes declined and eventually prices fell, too.

Lesson 13 - Comparative Advantage and Trade in a Global Economy

INTRODUCTION

Economics
Students (and many others) often assume incorrectly that trade is a zero-sum game: For every winner there must be a loser. The beauty of trade, and one of the most important points to get across in economics, is that trade is a win-win situation. Both parties must stand to gain, or they would not engage in voluntary trade. This basic concept applies to trade between individuals, as well as trade among regions or nations. Of course, no matter how great the advantages of free trade, there also will be disadvantages; there are no policies so good that everyone wins or so bad that everyone loses.

Students may have difficulty comprehending that one individual who can outperform another individual in every way may nevertheless be able to work out an advantageous trade or exchange with the less-competent person. Although the efficient person may be absolutely superior at everything (*absolute advantage*), the less-efficient person may be able to perform relatively better at some particular thing (*comparative advantage*) and therein lies the potential for advantageous exchange. The concept of comparative advantage forms the basis for voluntary exchange between individuals, as well as the basis for international trade.

Reasoning
Economic reasoning requires that people weigh costs and benefits of actions when they make decisions. This lesson enables the students to discover the benefits of specializing according to comparative advantage and to apply these concepts to international trade. Students also weigh advantages and disadvantages of free trade and trade restrictions by identifying winners and losers.

CONCEPTS
Absolute advantage
Barriers to trade
Comparative advantage
Opportunity cost
Specialization
Voluntary trade

CONTENT STANDARDS
5. Voluntary exchange occurs only when all participating parties expect to gain. This is true for trade among individuals or organizations within a nation, and among individuals or organizations in different nations.

6. When individuals, regions and nations specialize in what they can produce at the lowest cost and then trade with others, both production and consumption increase.

OBJECTIVES
Students will
1. Recognize and explain the difference between absolute advantage and comparative advantage.

2. Evaluate why a person with the absolute advantage in producing two services can nonetheless benefit from voluntary trade.

3. Identify winners and losers from free trade and restricted trade.

LESSON DESCRIPTION
Students observe or participate in a role-play situation in which one person is better at both of two activities. They complete a work sheet that leads to the conclusion that specialization and exchange make both people better off. Then they apply this situation to international trade and to the concepts of absolute advantage and comparative advantage. In small groups, they identify winners and losers from free trade and restricted trade.

TIME REQUIRED

60 minutes

MATERIALS

1. Visuals 13.1 and 13.2

2. Props for the Bert and Betsy role-play: apron, broom, dustpan, plastic dishes, dishcloth

3. A copy of Activities 13.1 and 13.2 for each student

PROCEDURE

1. Announce to the students that you want to explain a very important economic concept by telling a simple story. Select two students to role-play the parts of Bert and Betsy, and give them the props to use in their roles. Bert and Betsy do not need to speak in their roles; you may instruct them just to act out the parts while you read the story. (You may wish to select the students in advance and discuss their roles with them before class so they will be prepared.) Arrange the props on a desk or table in the front of the room.

2. Read the following story while the two students act out the roles of Bert and Betsy. Pause to allow Bert and Betsy to show their emotions, and for Betsy to show her skills and Bert to show his lack of skills, as appropriate.

Betsy and her brother Bert must help with the household chores before they may go out with their friends. Their job is twofold: First, they must wash and dry a sink full of dirty dishes that have accumulated for three days. Second, they must sweep up and take out three loads of trash from the garage, which hasn't been cleaned since the summer of 1998. Bert and Betsy's parents have announced that neither of them may go out until both jobs are completed. Both Bert and Betsy want to go out with their friends as soon as possible; this is their most important goal.

THE PREDICAMENT OF BERT AND BETSY

(Display Visual 13.1.) Betsy is a skilled, industrious, hard worker. In one hour, she can wash two sink loads of dishes by herself. Or in one hour she can sweep up and take out three loads of trash by herself. Poor Bert, on the other hand, appears to be a little incompetent when compared with his sister. Working by himself, in one hour he can wash one sink load of dishes. Or in one hour he could sweep up one load of trash. How should Bert and Betsy divide the work so they can go out with their friends as soon as possible? They are considering four options.

Option 1. The Parents' Plan: Bert and Betsy's parents suggest that they consider dividing the work by doing both jobs together. The parents think working together has the added benefit of helping Bert and Betsy get along better. First, the parents say, Bert and Betsy should both work on the dishes; then they should both tackle the sweeping. Betsy complains that this wouldn't be fair because Bert is a lazy slob and won't do his share of the work. However, she is willing to go along if this lets them finish sooner.

Option 2. Betsy's Plan: Betsy argues that they should divide the tasks and work separately. She says she should do the dishes because she likes this job better and, besides, Bert made most of the mess in the garage so he should sweep up all the trash.

Option 3. Bert's Plan: Bert argues that Betsy should do all the work. He suggests that this would be the most efficient option because she is so much faster and better at doing both jobs. He will just stay out of her way so he won't slow her down.

Option 4. Friend's Plan: Betsy's friend, who has just taken economics in school, tells them they are all wrong because each person should specialize in what he or she does best. The friend recommends that Betsy should do all the sweeping because, of the two jobs and compared with Bert, she is better at sweeping. Bert should do all the dishwashing because this is what he does best.

3. Thank Bert and Betsy for their performances. Give them a round of applause.

4. Distribute Activity 13.1 to the students, and ask them to answer the questions to evaluate the four options. They may do this individually or in small groups. Explain that in this example, when Bert and Betsy work together, they still work at the pace shown in the table. That is, they do not increase their individual productivity as a result of specialization.

5. When the students have finished answering the questions on Activity 13.1, call on students to give and explain their answers.
Part 1
   1. Who is better at cleaning dishes: Bert or Betsy? *Betsy*
   2. If Bert and Betsy work together, how many loads of dishes can they do in one hour? *Three loads*
   3. How many minutes would it take for them to wash one load of dishes working together? *20 minutes*
Show how you got your answer. *One hour divided by three loads of dishes*
   4. Who is better at sweeping up and taking out trash: Bert or Betsy? *Betsy*
   5. If Bert and Betsy work together, how many loads of trash can they do in one hour? *Four loads*
   6. How many minutes would it take for them to sweep up and take out three loads working together? *45 minutes*
Show how you got your answer. *They can do one load in 15 minutes or three loads in 45 minutes.*
Part 2
   Option 1. Time to complete one sink full of dishes: *20 minutes*
Time to complete three loads of trash: *45 minutes*
Time it would take for both to be finished: *65 minutes*

   Option 2. Time to complete one sink full of dishes: *30 minutes*
Time to complete three loads of trash: *3 hours*
Time it would take for both to be finished: *3 hours*
   Option 3. Time to complete one sink full of dishes: *30 minutes*
Time to complete three loads of trash: *1 hour*
Time it would take for both to be finished: *1 hour and 30 minutes*
   Option 4. Time to complete one sink full of dishes: *1 hour*
Time to complete three loads of trash: *1 hour*
Time it would take for both to be finished: *1 hour*

Which option is the most efficient: Which allows Betsy and Bert to complete the job in the shortest amount of time? *Option 4 allows both Bert and Betsy to finish in one hour, the shortest time of the four options and the shortest possible time for this example.*

OPPORTUNITY COST

6. Display Visual 13.2. Read the definitions with the students, and apply the concepts to Activity 13.1. Review the definition of opportunity cost as necessary. *Betsy had the absolute advantage in both washing dishes and sweeping trash. However, she had the comparative advantage only in sweeping trash, whereas Bert had the comparative advantage in washing dishes.*

   Opportunity cost is defined as the value of the next-best alternative that must be given up when scarce resources are used for one purpose instead of another. Technically, Betsy's opportunity cost of one load of trash is two-thirds of a load of dishes, whereas Bert's opportunity cost of one load of trash is one load of dishes.

   Betsy has the comparative advantage in sweeping trash, because she gives up less dishwashing than Bert. However, Betsy's opportunity cost of doing one load of dishes is 1.5 loads of trash, whereas Bert's opportunity cost of doing one load of dishes is one load of trash. Therefore, Bert has the comparative advantage in doing dishes because he gives up less trash sweeping than Betsy.

Although Betsy has the absolute advantage in both activities, she has the comparative advantage only in sweeping trash. Therefore, when Betsy and Bert specialize where each has the comparative advantage and work together (the equivalent of trading sweeping for dish washing), both are better off.

7. Ask the students to apply this example to international trade. Assume Bert is really the country of Bertonia and Betsy is really the country of Betswalia. Instead of sweeping trash and washing dishes, businesses in these countries are deciding whether to make cars or computers. How do the lessons of the Bert and Betsy example apply in this situation? *The lessons are the same. Even if one country such as Betswalia has the absolute advantage in both computers and cars, it should specialize where it has the comparative advantage and trade with the country that is the lowest-cost producer (has the comparative advantage) in producing the other product. This results in the efficient use of resources and benefits consumers in both countries.*

8. Tell the students that economists generally agree that specialization according to comparative advantage and free trade raises the overall standard of living in the countries involved. However, not everyone benefits from free trade. Because there are both winners and losers from free trade, sometimes governments decide to impose trade barriers or restrictions on free trade.

9. Distribute Activity 13.2. Working in groups of three or four, have the students identify winners and losers from the situations described.

10. When the students have finished, discuss their answers. *Answers to Activity 13.2 will vary. Possible answers are given here, but your students may also come up with other ideas.*
Part 1
   1. Which Americans are better off? Why? *Consumers. They have more cars to choose from, and competition may lead to lower prices of U.S. and Japanese cars.*
   2. Which Americans are worse off? Why? *Autoworkers. They may lose their jobs if U.S. consumers buy more Japanese cars and fewer U.S. cars.*
   3. Which Japanese are better off? Why? *Autoworkers. Demand for Japanese cars increases, so their wages may increase.*
   4. Which Japanese are worse off? Why? *Some consumers may have to pay higher prices for Japanese cars if the increase in demand for these cars in the United States raises their price in Japan.*
Part 2
Answers are essentially the opposite of those given for free trade.
   1. Which Americans are better off? Why? *Autoworkers*
   2. Which Americans are worse off? Why? *Consumers*
   3. Which Japanese are better off? Why? *Consumers of Japanese cars, if car prices fall in Japan because of decreased demand*
   4. Which Japanese are worse off? Why? *Autoworkers, if their wages fall because of decreased demand*

CLOSURE

Review the idea of comparative advantage
with the students, and discuss how specializing according to comparative advantage is the
basis for mutually beneficial trade. Emphasize
that although there are both winners and
losers from free trade, most economists are in
favor of free trade and agree that the benefits
to the winners outweigh the costs to the losers.

VISUAL 13.1
HOUSEHOLD CHORES

Household Chores (Output per hour)		
	Dishwashing (Number of sink loads)	**Sweeping** (Number of trash loads)
Betsy	2	3
Bert	1	1

VISUAL 13.2
ABSOLUTE AND COMPARATIVE ADVANTAGE

Absolute Advantage: the ability to produce more units of a good or service than some other producer using the same quantity of resources

Comparative Advantage: the ability to produce a good or service at a lower *opportunity cost* than another producer

Comparative Advantage is the economic basis for specialization and trade. If individuals and countries specialize in producing the goods in which they have the comparative advantage and trade for the goods in which others have the comparative advantage, both parties will be better off.

ACTIVITY 13.1
APPLYING COMPARATIVE ADVANTAGE

	Household Chores (Output per hour)	
	Dishwashing (Number of sink loads)	**Sweeping** (Number of trash loads)
Betsy	2	3
Bert	1	1

Part 1. The Predicament of Betsy and Bert

Betsy and her brother Bert must help with the household chores before they can go out with their friends. Their job is twofold:

   A. They must wash and dry one sink full of dirty dishes that accumulated for three days.

   B. They must sweep up and take out three loads of trash from the garage, which hasn't been cleaned since the summer of 1998.

Bert and Betsy's parents have announced that neither of them may go out until both jobs are completed. Both Bert and Betsy want to go out with their friends as soon as possible. As shown in the table, Betsy can wash two sink loads of dishes in one hour, or she can sweep up and take out three loads of trash. Bert can wash one sink load of dishes in one hour, or he can sweep up and take out one load of trash. (Assume that if Bert and Betsy work together, they still work at the pace shown in the table.) Answer the questions below to determine how Bert and Betsy can complete both jobs in the shortest amount of time.

1.   Who is better at cleaning dishes: Bert or Betsy?

2.   If Bert and Betsy work together, how many loads of dishes can they do in one hour?

3.   How many minutes would it take for them to wash one load of dishes working together? Show how you got your answer.

4.   Who is better at sweeping up and taking out trash: Bert or Betsy?

5.   If Bert and Betsy work together, how many loads of trash can they do in one hour?

6.   How many minutes would it take for them to sweep up and take out three loads working together? Show how you got your answer.

ACTIVITY 13.1, continued
APPLYING COMPARATIVE ADVANTAGE

Part 2. Analyzing the Options

Now that you have worked with the data, it is time to use this information to make a decision. Read each of the options below. Answer the questions to determine the total amount of time it would take to complete the job of sweeping up and taking out three loads of trash and washing one sink full of dishes.

Option 1. The Parents' Plan: Bert and Betsy's parents suggest that they consider dividing the tasks by working together on both jobs. First they should both work on the dishes, then they should both tackle the sweeping. Betsy complains that this wouldn't be fair because Bert is a lazy slob and won't do his share of the work. However, she is willing to go along if this allows them to finish sooner.

Time to complete one sink full of dishes: _____

Time to complete three loads of trash: _____

Time it would take for both to be finished: _____

Option 2. Betsy's Plan: Betsy argues that they should divide up the tasks and work separately. She says she should do the dishes because she likes this job better and, besides, Bert made most of the mess in the garage so he should clean up the trash.

Time to complete one sink full of dishes: _____

Time to complete three loads of trash: _____

Time it would take for both to be finished: _____

Option 3. Bert's Plan: Bert argues that Betsy should do all the work. He suggests that this would be the most efficient option because she is so much faster and better at doing both jobs.

Time to complete one sink full of dishes: _____

Time to complete three loads of trash: _____

Time it would take for both to be finished: _____

Option 4. Friend's Plan: Betsy's friend, who has just taken economics in school, tells them they are all wrong because each person should specialize in what he or she does best. She recommends that Betsy should do all the sweeping because, of the two jobs and compared with Bert, she is better at sweeping. Bert should do all the dishwashing because this is what he does best.

Time to complete one sink full of dishes: _____

Time to complete three loads of trash: _____

Time it would take for both to be finished: _____

Which option is the most efficient: which allows Betsy and Bert to complete the job in the shortest amount of time? Explain.

ACTIVITY 13.2
WINNERS AND LOSERS FROM FREE TRADE
AND TRADE RESTRICTIONS

The United States produces cars and it also imports cars from other countries. Using the decision to import cars from Japan as an example, first try to identify winners and losers from free trade. Then try to identify winners and losers when we place restrictions on trade or charge foreign companies money (a tariff or tax on imports) to bring their goods into this country. Briefly explain your answers in the spaces provided.

Part 1: Free Trade
Assume there are no limits to the number of Japanese cars that Japanese companies may sell in the United States and that the United States doesn't charge any tariffs to Japanese companies that sell Japanese cars in this country.

1. Which Americans are better off? Why?

2. Which Americans are worse off? Why?

3. Which Japanese are better off? Why?

4. Which Japanese are worse off? Why?

Part 2: Restricted Trade
Assume the United States now charges Japanese car companies a tariff to sell their cars in this country and also limits the total number of Japanese cars they may import.

1. Which Americans are better off? Why?

2. Which Americans are worse off? Why?

3. Which Japanese are better off? Why?

4. Which Japanese are worse off? Why?

Lesson 14 - Exchange Rates: Money Around the World

INTRODUCTION

Economics

Because different countries use different currencies, international trade requires an organized system for exchanging money among nations. If an American wants to buy goods produced in Japan, somewhere along the line dollars must be exchanged for yen. An *exchange rate* is the price of one nation's currency in terms of another nation's currency. Exchange rates may be *fixed* (prevented from rising and falling with changes in the supply and demand for the currency) or *flexible* (free to float with changes in the supply and demand for the currency). Today the world's major currencies are flexible (floating), but nations sometimes intervene to try to manage exchange rates. A change in exchange rates may have a significant effect on the flow of trade among nations and on a nation's domestic economy. Many factors affect exchange rates including changes in preferences for foreign goods, relative incomes, inflation, interest rates, and speculation on future values of foreign exchange.

Reasoning

Students who have traveled in other countries or who come from other countries have direct experience with exchange rates but may not have thought about the issues underlying the purposes of these rates and their fluctuations. An important lesson in economics is understanding that forces of supply and demand affect the value of major currencies, which, in turn, affects prices of goods and services and trade among nations.

CONCEPTS

Exchange rates
Fixed exchange rates
Flexible (floating) exchange rates
Foreign-exchange markets
Supply and demand for foreign currency

CONTENT STANDARDS

7. Markets exist when buyers and sellers interact. This interaction determines market prices and thereby allocates scarce goods and services.

11. Money makes it easier to trade, borrow, save, invest and compare the value of goods and services.

INSTRUCTIONAL OBJECTIVES

Students will

1. Participate in auctions that demonstrate the role of foreign currency in buying goods from other countries.

2. Define exchange rates and understand that the forces of supply and demand determine flexible exchange rates.

3. Calculate the prices of U.S. goods in foreign currencies whose value changes over time, and explain the role exchange rates have in the price differences.

LESSON DESCRIPTION

Students participate in two auctions to demonstrate the determination of flexible exchange rates and the need for foreign currency to purchase goods from other countries. In the first auction, the students may buy goods produced only in their own countries. In the second auction, the students may buy foreign goods but must first exchange currency in order to do so. They discuss the results of the auctions and the average rate of exchange between the two forms of money used in the auctions. Students then participate in a small-group activity to determine the price of a bundle of American-made goods in Japanese yen, Canadian dollars and British pounds during two time periods.

TIME REQUIRED

75 minutes

MATERIALS

1. Visual 14.1

2. A package of macaroni and a package of beans to use as money, and small plastic bags. (If the macaroni breaks easily, use two different colors of beans or another item such as paper clips.) Prepare money packages before class by putting 100 pieces of macaroni into one small plastic bag and 200 beans into another small plastic bag.
    (Optional) Prepare two bags each of 100 pieces of macaroni and 200 beans for use in each auction.

3. Twelve valuable items to be auctioned as follows: Four items should be the same and there should be two each of the other four items, which should be different. For example, you could have four school pencils, two library passes, two cards worth 10 extra-credit points each, two chocolate candy bars and two peanut candy bars. (You may use pictures of goods or slips of paper with the name of a good on them instead.)

4. A large amount of two different desirable items such as peanuts and small candies (or slips of paper naming two desirable items). One of these items is for Country A and the other is for Country B. For a class of 30, you need about 50 to 100 of each item to be safe.

5. A copy of Activity 14.1 for each student

6. **(Optional)** Small prizes for the students serving as country leaders

PROCEDURE

AUCTION 1

1. Announce that the class will participate in an auction activity to better understand how money and prices are related through markets.
    A. Divide the class down the middle of the room into two groups of approximately equal size. (If more students are sitting on one side of the room than the other, you may tell a few to immigrate to the other side for the activity.)
    B. Tell the groups they are residents of two neighboring countries that do not permit citizens to trade with each other. One side of the room, Country A, uses macaroni for money. The other side of the room, Country B, uses beans for money.
    C. Quickly distribute the 100 pieces of macaroni and the 200 beans to the students in their respective countries while continuing to discuss the auctions.
    Note: If you have 30 students, the 15 students in Country A will average about six to seven pieces of macaroni each, and the 15 students in Country B will average about 13 to 14 beans each. Do not distribute the money equally within each country; for example, some students in Country B could have five or six beans while others have 20.

2. Tell the students the macaroni and beans represent income that residents of Country A and Country B earned during the past year. They may use the income to purchase goods and services produced in their countries.
    A. Show the goods that are produced by Country A, for example, a library pass, a school pencil, a chocolate candy bar and a large supply of peanuts. List the goods on the board.
    B. Show the goods produced by Country B, for example, a card good for 10 extra-credit points, a school pencil (identical to the one in Country A), a peanut candy bar and a large supply of small candies. List the goods on the board.

C. Point out that both countries produce one good that is the same (school pencils) but each also produces goods that are unique. Because trade is not allowed, people in Country B cannot purchase the goods that are produced in Country A and vice versa.

3. Appoint leaders for each country and have them stand in front of their countries with the items representing goods their country produced in the past year. Explain that the job of the leaders is to auction off to the highest bidders the three valuable goods for macaroni in Country A and beans in Country B. Leaders will not take part in the auctions themselves. Students who do not get one of the three more valuable items will exchange their income for the small candy or peanuts so everyone will end up with something. Students may not save their bean or macaroni income. **Note:** Choose leaders carefully! They need to conduct the auctions quickly, help distribute candy or peanuts to the students who didn't get the three auctioned items, and collect all the beans or macaroni after the first auction. Tell them this should be done in about 10 minutes or less.

Ask if there are any questions. The students may comment that the income distribution was unfair. You may respond yes, and this is often true in real life, too. They may say they want to buy something from the other country. Point out that this is a problem with trade barriers. The leaders may complain that they can't take part in the auctions, so they will automatically end up with one of the less desirable items. Respond that politicians often don't make a lot of money, or tell them they will receive a small prize or extra-credit points for their work later.

4. Have the leaders conduct the auctions for their countries at the same time. You may want to have one stand in the front of the room and the other in the back of the room to eliminate confusion about who is

bidding for what. (The auctions may be done sequentially, but this can be very time-consuming.)

5. After the auctions, the leaders should pass out the candy or peanuts to anyone with money in their country. You may want to ask other students to help so this goes quickly. Make sure all the bean money and macaroni money is collected and returned to you.

6. When both groups have finished:
   A. Ask what prices the students paid (in beans and macaroni) for the three auctioned items. Record the prices on the board.
   B. Point out that one of the items (pencils) was the same in both countries. Compare the prices students paid for it in beans and macaroni. *Probably the bean price was higher because there were more beans in circulation.*
   C. Probably bean prices were higher in general than macaroni prices. Ask why this was so. *There were more beans than macaroni in circulation.*
   D. Ask whether people in Country B were richer than people in Country A because there were more beans than macaroni. *The correct answer is no. The amount of money in circulation in a country does not make the country wealthier. What is important is how much the incomes will buy in different countries. This activity does not show that either country is wealthier. However, some individuals within the countries were wealthier because they had higher incomes than others.*

AUCTION 2

7. Tell the students a year has passed and many things have not changed. The leaders are still in power (assuming they did a good job – or you could replace them). The goods produced in each country are the same. Display goods identical to those in the first auction. Country A still uses mac-

aroni money and Country B still uses bean money. Quickly distribute beans and macaroni as before. (Average amounts will be the same in each country because you still have 100 pieces of macaroni and 200 beans for the same number of students. However, different students should have different amounts if you distribute it randomly.)

8. Announce that one important thing has changed: The governments of the two countries now permit people in one country to buy goods in the other country. However, anyone who wants to buy something in Country A needs macaroni, and anyone who wants to buy something in Country B needs beans. Therefore, before the auctions, you will give them time to exchange beans and macaroni if they wish to do so. There is no fixed exchange rate. Students with beans will try to trade for as much macaroni as possible, and students with macaroni will try to trade for as many beans as possible. No one has to exchange currency if they don't want to.

9. Write Beans at the top of one column on the board and Macaroni at the top of another column. Tell the students that if they decide to exchange currency, they must report the completed transaction amount to you. For example, if they trade seven beans for three macaroni, you would write 7 in the bean column and 3 in the macaroni column. Ask if there are any questions. Give the students five to 10 minutes to trade currency.

10. At the end of the currency-trading period, tell the leaders to conduct the auctions (quickly) as before. This time, however, buyers may go to whichever country they choose. (Usually most students have a majority of money from one country or the other. However, a few students may ask what to do if they have currency from both countries and want to bid on items from both places. Instruct them to do what they think is best. Tell them that competition

often occurs between buyers, and they can't always get what they want when they want it. Alternatively, you could conduct the auctions one at a time, but this can be time-consuming.)

11. When the auctions are finished, let the students exchange their remaining beans or macaroni for the small candy or peanuts as appropriate.

DISCUSSION

12. Record on the board the prices of the goods in each country from the second auctions, and discuss the changes in prices between the two rounds. *The sales prices in beans were probably still higher than in macaroni since more beans were in circulation in both auctions. However, relative prices may have changed: Popular goods may have had higher prices in the second auction since there were more potential buyers.*

13. Using Visual 14.1, discuss exchange rates and trade among nations.

WHAT IS AN EXCHANGE RATE?
   A. Define exchange rates as the price or value of one nation's currency in terms of another nation's currency.
   B. Ask the students if they have had experiences with exchange rates. *Answers will vary, but they may mention exchanging dollars for foreign currency when traveling in another country.*
   C. Determine the exchange rate in the auction activity. Go to the board where you recorded the beans and macaroni exchanged in the activity and total the amounts in each column (e.g., 62 macaroni and 119 beans). Divide these amounts to get the average exchange rate used in the game (for example, 62/119 = .52, and 119/62 = 1.9). Rounding, the exchange rate was one-half macaroni for one bean or two beans for one macaroni. Assuming the goods available in both countries were

desirable to the students, the exchange rates often are close to 2:1 in this activity because there were twice as many beans in circulation as macaroni.

WHY DO PEOPLE IN ONE COUNTRY WANT CURRENCY FROM ANOTHER COUNTRY?

Ask the students why they wanted the other country's currency in the activity. *Some citizens of Country A wanted beans, and some citizens of Country B wanted macaroni to buy goods that were not available in their countries.* This reason is true in real life also. Other reasons for wanting currency from another country include traveling to another country or investing in the assets of another country (for example, wanting to buy stock in a German corporation or real estate in Costa Rica). Some people want foreign currency because they think it may be more stable or safe than their country's currency. Others want it for speculative reasons: They hope to make a profit if the value of currency changes.

WHAT IS A FLEXIBLE (FLOATING) EXCHANGE RATE?

Explain that when exchange rates are flexible, values are determined by the supply and demand for various currencies. In the activity, exchange rates were flexible because the students could exchange money at whatever rate they wanted. Today the major currencies in the world are flexible to a large extent. (However, governments sometimes try to buy and sell large amounts of a nation's currency to try to influence exchange rates, so the system is often called a *managed float.*)

WHAT IS A FIXED EXCHANGE RATE?

Explain that when exchange rates are fixed, the government sets the rate at which one country's money may be exchanged for another country's money. In the activity, if you had announced that the students could exchange two of their beans for one macaroni and no other

amount, this would have been an example of a fixed exchange rate.

WHY DO FLEXIBLE EXCHANGE RATES CHANGE?

Explain that flexible exchange rates change frequently over time: over years, months, weeks and even during a given day. The reasons can be related to supply and demand. (Part of this answer is relatively advanced. For average classes, you may wish to briefly discuss supply and demand and focus on reason A: changes in preferences for foreign goods.)

Economists often cite the following factors for changes in exchange rates:

A. Changes in preferences for foreign goods. For example, if Americans want to buy more goods from Japan, they will demand more Japanese yen (and supply more U.S. dollars in exchange for the yen). The dollar/yen exchange rate would change and the yen would be worth more dollars (and the dollar would be worth fewer yen).

B. Changes in prices in different countries. For example, if Russia has high inflation compared with the United States, Russian goods would become more expensive compared with U.S. goods. Russians would demand more U.S. dollars to buy cheaper U.S. goods (and supply more Russian rubles in exchange for the dollars). The dollar/ruble exchange rate would change and the dollar would be worth more rubles (and the ruble would be worth fewer dollars).

C. Changes in interest rates in different countries. For example, if you could earn 10 percent on a savings account in Europe and only three percent on a savings account in the United States, Americans would want to supply their dollars and demand more euros in order to deposit their money in a European bank. The dollar/euro exchange rate would change and the euro would be worth more dollars (and the dollar would be worth fewer euros).

D. Changes in incomes in different

countries. For example, if incomes in the United States were increasing compared with those in Mexico, people in the United States could afford to buy more Mexican goods and more U.S. goods as well. Demand for pesos would go up, and the supply of dollars would increase in exchange for pesos. The dollar/peso exchange rate would change and the dollar would be worth fewer pesos (and the peso would be worth more dollars).

E. Speculation. For example, if many people think the dollar will increase in value compared with the euro, they will buy (demand) dollars today (and supply euros) in hopes of selling the dollars back at higher prices later. The dollar/euro exchange rate would change, and the dollar would be worth more euros (and the euro would be worth fewer dollars).

GROUP ACTIVITY

14. Distribute Activity 14.1, "Working With Foreign Exchange Rates." Divide the students into small groups to answer the questions. To help the students get started, you may want to go over how to convert dollars to another currency using data from the table from 1998 and 2000. For example, if an item cost $10 in the United States in 1998, it would have cost 1,309.9 yen ($10 times 130.99), 14.8 Canadian dollars ($10 times 1.48) and 6.9 British pounds ($10 times .69). If an item cost $10 in the United States in 2000, it would have cost 1,077.3 yen, 14.8 Canadian dollars and 6.8 British pounds.

15. Discuss the answers to the questions in Activity 14.1.

1. It is 1996. Sara is watching her favorite video, wearing her favorite sweatshirt and eating a sandwich. She paid $15.98 for the video, $30 for the sweatshirt and $1.99 for the sandwich.
   A. What were Sara's total expenditures for the three goods? *$47.97*
   B. How many yen would a Japanese

tourist have exchanged to purchase the same products? *5,218.18 yen*
   C. How many Canadian dollars would a Canadian tourist have exchanged? *65.24 Canadian dollars*
   D. How many pounds would a British tourist have exchanged? *30.70 British pounds*

2. It is 2002, and prices of the three goods have not changed in the United States.
   A. What are the new prices in Japanese yen? *5,952.60 yen*
   B. What are the new prices in Canadian dollars? *73.87 Canadian dollars*
   C. What are the new prices in British pounds? *33.10 British pounds*

3. Describe what happened to the amounts the tourists would spend in 2002 compared with the amounts they spent in 1996 in each of the foreign currencies. *In 2002, tourists would have to spend more Japanese yen, more Canadian dollars and more British pounds compared with 1996 to buy the same goods. Although the prices of the goods stayed the same in the United States, the prices people paid in foreign currency changed because of changes in exchange rates.*

4. According to the figures in the table, what happened to the value of the U.S. dollar compared with the Japanese yen between 1996 and 1998, 1998 and 2000, and 2000 and 2002? *Between 1996 and 1998, the value of the dollar rose, or appreciated, relative to the yen (the dollar could be exchanged for more yen in 1998 than in 1996).*
   Between 1998 and 2000, the value of the dollar fell, or depreciated, relative to the yen (the dollar could be exchanged for fewer yen in 2000 than in 1998). Between 2000 and 2002, the value of the dollar rose, or appreciated, relative to the yen.
   Note that this could also be

expressed by saying that the value of the yen fell (depreciated) relative to the dollar between 1996 and 1998, rose (appreciated) between 1998 and 2000 and fell (depreciated) between 2000 and 2002.

CLOSURE

Review the major points of the auctions and Activity 14.1 with the students.

1. Different countries use different currencies.

2. To buy something in or from another country, you generally need currency from the other country. One of the reasons currencies are exchanged among countries is because people want to buy something that isn't available in their country.

3. Currencies are traded in foreign-exchange markets. In the auction activity, the exchange rates were determined by supply and demand or by the students who wanted currency from the other country. This simulated a flexible exchange-rate system. Exchange rates for major currencies in the world today are largely flexible.

4. If the teacher had set the exchange rate at, for example, two beans for one macaroni, this would have simulated a fixed exchange-rate system.

5. Changes in exchange rates cause prices of imported goods to change, even when the prices of the goods haven't changed in the country where the goods were produced.

FOLLOW-UP ACTIVITIES

1. Have the students look up current exchange rates in newspapers and practice converting back and forth among yen, dollars and euros.

2. Make up an international shopping list of items from countries other than the United States and Japan. Price the items in their own currencies. Have the students figure out the cost for each item in dollars and in yen.

VISUAL 14.1
QUESTIONS ABOUT EXCHANGE RATES

What is an exchange rate?

Why do people in one country want currency from another country?

What is a flexible (floating) exchange rate?

What is a fixed exchange rate?

Why do flexible exchange rates change?

ACTIVITY 14.1
WORKING WITH FOREIGN EXCHANGE RATES

The United States uses dollars for money. When people from other countries want to buy goods and services from U.S. firms, they must pay in U.S. dollars. When Americans want to buy foreign products, they must pay in foreign money. People and businesses get the foreign money they need by buying it in foreign-exchange markets. *Foreign-exchange markets* are like other markets in many ways, except instead of buying and selling goods and services, people buy and sell money from different countries. In terms of supply and demand, Americans who want to buy goods from other countries create a demand for foreign currency. People in other countries who want to buy goods from the United States supply their currency in exchange for dollars.

The following table shows exchange rates among the American dollar, the Japanese yen, the Canadian dollar and the British pound from 1996 through 2002.

Year	Japanese yen per U.S. dollar	Canadian dollar per U.S. dollar	British pound per U.S. dollar
1996	108.78	1.36	.64
1998	130.99	1.48	.69
2000	107.73	1.48	.68
2002	124.09	1.54	.69

(Sources: Data for 1996-2000: Economic Report of the President, 2001, Table B-110. Data for 2002: New York Times, May 22, 2002. 2000 figures are for third quarter. 2002 figures are for May 21, 2002.)

1. It is 1996. Sara is watching her favorite video, wearing her favorite sweatshirt and eating a sandwich. She paid $15.98 for the video, $30 for the sweatshirt and $1.99 for the sandwich.
    A. What were Sara's total expenditures for the three goods?

    B. How many yen would a Japanese tourist have exchanged to purchase the same products?

    C. How many Canadian dollars would a Canadian tourist have exchanged?

    D. How many pounds would a British tourist have exchanged?

2. It is 2002, and prices of the three goods have not changed in the United States.
    A. What are the new prices in Japanese yen?

    B. What are the new prices in Canadian dollars?

    C. What are the new prices in British pounds?

3. Describe what happened to the amounts the tourists would spend in 2002 compared with the amounts they spent in 1996 in each of the foreign currencies.

4. According to the figures in the table, what happened to the value of the U.S. dollar compared with the Japanese yen between 1996 and 1998, 1998 and 2000, and 2000 and 2002?